PUFFIN STOR[...]

Edited by Elea[...]

PS8[...]

ENJOYING PA[...]

A. C. WARD

Everyone needs help at first in looking at
pictures, for a good artist does not set down
exactly what he sees, as it would be recorded
by a camera. He has not merely sight, but
vision. He uses imagination in creating what
you look at on the canvas, so we have to
learn to look at the picture so as to share that
vision, and to understand what the artist
saw in his mind's eye when he painted it.

In this book you will find the story of
painting in Europe from prehistoric times to
modern painters like Picasso and Paul Nash.
The text is easy to read and will help to form
a sense of values, to pick your own favourites,
and to know why you enjoy them more than
other pictures. It is written with authority
and enthusiasm, and is illustrated with
photographs of famous pictures.

Enjoying Paintings

BY

A. C. WARD

PENGUIN BOOKS

Penguin Books Ltd, Harmondsworth, Middlesex

U.S.A.: Penguin Books Inc., 3300 Clipper Mill Road, Baltimore 11, Md
[*Educational Representative :*
D. C. Heath & Co, 285 Columbus Avenue, Boston 16, Mass]

CANADA: Penguin Books (Canada) Ltd, 47 Green Street,
Saint Lambert, Montreal, P.Q.

AUSTRALIA: Penguin Books Pty Ltd, 762 Whitehorse Road,
Mitcham, Victoria

SOUTH AFRICA: Penguin Books (S.A.) Pty Ltd, Gibraltar House,
Regents Road, Sea Point, Cape Town

—

First published 1949
Published by Penguin Books 1954

Made and printed in Great Britain
by Hunt, Barnard & Co., Ltd, Aylesbury
Collogravure plates
by Harrison & Sons Ltd

CONTENTS

PLATES

ACKNOWLEDGEMENTS

Permission to reproduce illustrations is gratefully acknowledged to the following: The Jules Bache Collection, New York, for *Don Manuel Osorio de Zuñiga* by Goya; the Ashmolean Museum, Oxford, for the Prehistoric Hunting Scene; Eileen Tristram for the painting from Canterbury Cathedral of *Elizabeth and the Child John;* The Courtauld Institute for the loan of reproductions in the Witt Library; Mr V. W. Van Gogh for *The Blossoming Peartree* by Vincent Van Gogh; Edward James Esq. and Mrs Paul Nash for *Encounter in the Afternoon* by Paul Nash. The paintings in the National Gallery are reproduced by courtesy of the Trustees, the National Gallery, London, and those in the Tate Gallery are reproduced by courtesy of the Trustees of the Tate Gallery, London.

I

Seeing Into Things

IF you had been living many thousands of years ago instead of in the present century, your father would have spent much of his time in searching for food, instead of in earning money to buy it. He would have been a hunter and you would have listened at the end of the day to the men of your family or tribe telling (sometimes singing) stories of their adventures while tracking wild animals. Those stories might have been true, or partly true, or not true at all, according to whether the tellers wanted to boast of their courage and skill, and whether their imagination was lively or dull.

Those who were what we now call 'imaginative' would speak one or other or both of two different kinds of truth: the truth which is concerned with facts – the things we see with our eyes and hear with our ears; and the other kind of truth – often more 'real' and interesting and exciting than facts – which belongs to the things that come into our minds from nowhere, but may nevertheless be of greater value to ourselves than the objects we can see and touch. We all know that pleasant world of make-believe in which many of our happiest hours are spent when we are young. Grown-ups sometimes scold us about it, calling us day-dreamers, or accusing us of falsehood when we speak of our adventures there. As we grow up we usually find it harder and harder to keep in touch with the make-believe land where we used to feel so much at home.

What happens to us to bring about this change?

Our bodies and minds develop and alter; we have to think about 'serious' matters, such as passing examinations and earning a living; we are expected to become reasonable instead of imaginative. Reasonable people are sensible and

9

hard-headed enough to 'get on in the world'; they are tough; they go into business and make money.

BORN TO BE ARTISTS

But there are people who do not become like that when they grow up. Though outwardly they may appear to be the same as others, inwardly they are quite different. They are not tough, but sensitive; not reasonable, but imaginative; not hard-headed, but 'unpractical'. They hate doing the things that most other adults don't mind doing, such as catching the same train every morning to the City and passing most part of their lives cooped up in workshops or offices. They are the people born to be artists – poets, novelists, musicians, actors, sculptors, painters. That doesn't mean that they work less hard than the practical business men. Far from it. Art is not a soft job. An artist's work is never done. He doesn't expect a seven-hour day or a five-day week or an annual holiday with pay. If an artist divides his earnings by the number of hours he works, he may very well find that he is worse off in pocket than a postman or a charwoman. Some artists, of course, happen also to be very good business men, and get on in the world as well as if they were bankers. Most of them, however, are not much interested in money and are content with little if only they can remain free to write, or compose music, or paint; remain free, that is to say, to do the work they are certain they were born to do. No genuine artist *chooses* to be an artist; he is compelled to become one by some force inside himself which drives him on and will not let him rest until he obeys its will, even though obedience may result in his being neglected and poverty-stricken and suffering heart-breaking disappointment. That is not a romantic experience; yet, even so, no genuine artist would think his life wasted, nor would he wish to follow any other profession if he could have a second chance and live all over again.

Nearly every artist feels more at home in his own private

world of make-believe – the world of the imagination – than in the everyday world of fact. But we must take care not to make the very common mistake of supposing that the world of imagination is at the opposite pole to the world of reality. Poets, who are artists in words, have sometimes 'imagined' things that scientists long afterwards discovered to be real; and one reason why artists are valuable members of any community, even when they are despised by the practical folk, is that imagination serves them as a sort of combined mental searchlight and X-ray apparatus, enabling them to see farther and look deeper than most of us can. An X-ray plate makes visible to our eyes things we might otherwise be certain are not there or are entirely different. So let us not be in a hurry to declare that a painter is in the wrong if he makes familiar objects look unfamiliar. Whereas most of us see only the outward appearances of people and things, an artist is able to penetrate into and beyond. We have *sight* – we see what is visible. An artist has *vision* – he sees both the visible and the invisible.

EYES ARE OPENED

So true is this that if when we look at a picture it all appears very much the same as what we see for ourselves in the world round about us, the chances are that it is the work of a not-very-good artist. After all, why should we bother to spend time looking at pictures if they show us nothing more than we can see by using our own eyes when we look at nature? It is healthier to go for a country walk than to stare at a landscape painting which looks exactly like country scenery. But it is very well worth while looking at a landscape painting if our eyes are opened, when next we walk in the country, to things we should not otherwise have noticed. A landscape painting might, for example, make us aware for the first time of the lovely shapes of bare trees in winter, though we might until then have thought of them as black and uninteresting, not worth looking at again until the buds and leaves come back.

Once we begin to enjoy the shapes of trees, however, a new world of delight opens to us: we have begun to take pleasure in *structural form*, which is not easily detected from the outside; it is usually hidden beneath the surfaces of things, and we have to learn to look *into* them rather than only to look *at* them. So this is one new source of pleasure that an artist can lead us to. Going back to our tree, we shall not only enjoy its form in winter when it is bare, we shall also enjoy it twofold in summer because we shall have learned to see the permanently beautiful body (as it were) of the tree beneath its beautiful seasonal clothing of leaves, and of flowers and fruit if it is that kind of tree. We shall have learned something else too. From that moment, whenever we look at a landscape painting with trees in full leaf or flower, we shall notice whether the painter has got the structural form (or anatomy) of the tree correct below its summer clothing. And from that we shall go on to notice whether a portrait painter has got his sitter's anatomy right. Some artists are good at what is called 'flesh painting', which consists in showing the beauty of skin colour and texture, yet not so good at making us feel that the *bones* of the person are right.

PICTURES IN CAVES

We might seem to have wandered far from the prehistoric hunter and his companions telling stories round the fire at the end of the day, but we have intentionally set out on a preliminary ramble; so we can go with an easy mind down any promising side lane before we set out in earnest on our main road.

All story-telling soon turns from plain and straightforward statements about actual happenings into the telling of invented tales; and in Early Man this kind of invention, born of imagination and vision, must have developed rapidly.

Art is born as soon as imagination quickens, and hunting and verbal descriptions of hunting would not for long remain interesting enough in themselves to satisfy even our remotest ancestors. When they retreated for shelter into the depths of their caves they began to do what children still do: that is, to make pictures on the walls, and on the ceilings when they could reach them. You will probably be severely scolded if you draw on your bedroom walls or elsewhere indoors – and indeed it is a messy habit in a modern house – though you will have been obeying a primitive urge which people young and old have felt from earliest times, the urge to decorate bare surfaces.

It is only to be expected that when Early Man took to drawing on walls and scratching on pieces of bone he should have begun with pictures of the animals and hunting scenes which were so important in his daily life. Many cave-paintings have lasted in good condition from the Stone Age down to the present day, and there are particularly fine examples in France and Spain, the best-known being those accidently discovered in 1880 by the little daughter of a professor at Altamira, near Santander, in the north of Spain. These paintings were done on walls deep inside the caves, far beyond the limit to which daylight could penetrate, and it is hard to believe that they could ever have been painted in such difficult conditions and in what must have been a very feeble artificial light from crude stone lamps fed with animal fat. Yet there they are still – pictures of bison and other huge creatures, wonderfully drawn and coloured with red, brown, and black earth; pictures which a trained present-day artist could be proud of.

SEEING THE INVISIBLE

One of the most interesting things about these cave-paintings is that although they are the work of primitive man (supposed to have been himself not far above the brutes), they raise questions which still interest us to-day: questions concerning the relation between outward fact and inward truth, between the visible and the invisible, between sight (the ability to see with the outward eye) and vision (the power of seeing with the inward eye or imagination). We have said that *an artist sees both the visible and the invisible*, which must seem an oddly extravagant statement to those who have not met it before. We had better consider it further.

In his famous ode on *Intimations of Immortality from Recollections of Early Childhood* Wordsworth wrote:

> There was a time when meadow, grove, and stream,
>   The earth, and every common sight,
>   To me did seem
>   Apparell'd in celestial light,
> The glory and the freshness of a dream.

He goes on to say that 'heaven lies about us in our infancy', but that the veil of earthly life comes down and thickens more and more about us as we grow older and become increasingly occupied with everyday affairs, so that the celestial light dwindles until

> At length the Man perceives it die away,
> And fade into the light of common day.

But even while Wordsworth was writing those lines, which are true of nearly all of us, there was living another English poet of whom they were not true.

That poet, William Blake, was also a painter and engraver, and there has never been anyone else quite like him. In many ways he was a fairly ordinary person, for although it is true to say that he was in close touch with heaven all his life through, he had plenty of average common sense, was an excellent craftsman at his trade of engraving, and lived very happily with his wife from the day they married until the day he died forty-five years later (in 1827) at the age of all but seventy. He was interested in public affairs and, though he had little money and was sometimes in need, he had good friends whom he valued far more than money. From a practical, worldly point of view he would no doubt be considered a failure, and it was not until long after his death that he was recognized as a great man and a unique genius. One of his sayings can be taken as the key to Blake himself: 'A fool sees not the same tree that a wise man sees.'

'A TREE FILLED WITH ANGELS'

Blake was undoubtedly a wise man, and what he saw when he looked around him was certainly not the same as other men saw, whether they were fools or sages. When he was about eight years old he saw on Peckham Rye (then a countrified spot, now swallowed up in a drab desert of houses in south-east London) 'a tree filled with angels, bright angelic wings bespangling every bough like stars'. When he reached home and spoke about this he only narrowly escaped a thrashing from his father. But no amount of thrashing could have kept him from seeing visions; and no amount of hard common sense in our opinion about him can disprove that throughout his life he was in touch with a world which is closed to ordinary persons. 'I hear a voice you cannot hear . . . I see a hand you cannot see', he wrote to a friend; and the more we know about Blake the more certain we are that he was telling the plain truth. He died in a back room in Lambeth – died so peacefully that even his devoted wife by his bedside scarcely noticed his going – and 'Just before he died his countenance became fair – his eyes brightened and he burst out singing of the things he saw in heaven.'

Happily for us, Blake revealed in many of his drawings and paintings the visions he saw so often: visions of angels and other celestial beings, filling his pictures with a spirit which is both mystical and natural. Though we may never see such things for ourselves, there are lines by a later poet, Francis Thompson, which express our certainty that Blake's works of vision and imagination bring us face to face with divine truth and eternal reality:

> O world invisible, we view thee,
> O world intangible, we touch thee,
> O world unknowable, we know thee. . . .

The extent to which an artist uses the inward eye of imagination varies according to the kind of person he is and the kind of work he has to do. Blake, being a visionary, used imagination to the full; it was second nature to him to believe and trust his inward eye. Yet Blake was an extremely rare sort of person and a law unto himself, so when we talk about an artist's imagination we must not expect to find it always brimming over so unmistakably as it did in Blake. This is just as well for us. Much of Blake's work is far from easy to understand, and as most of us are far more earth-bound than he was, we are likely to prefer pictures of earthly subjects.

We have already seen that an artist who paints a tree in its winter bareness may make us aware for the first time of a kind of beauty our own eyes had missed, though it was there all the while. But such an artist has not performed any·important imaginative feat for us. He has simply shown us how much more interesting and attractive – how much more fun – the world can be if our eyes are fully open to what is round about us in the world of fact. Blake, on the other hand, offers us perhaps nine-tenths vision and imagination and only one-tenth fact.

AN ARTIST SEES BENEATH THE SURFACE

There is another kind of artist who depicts familiar objects in a way that gives them something very like their ordinary appearance, yet as we look more attentively we become aware that we are not only seeing the subject of the picture, we are also feeling the mood or spirit of it. The painting is, as it were, telling us more than we knew before about that particular person or object. It is as though the surface of the picture is able to become transparent, so that we can see what is going on inside whatever it is that the artist has painted. To take an example: you may be friendly for years with a particular person and think you know him or her very well. Then one day you are shown a portrait-painting of that person. As you look at the picture, you realize that it is not only a 'face-painting' (the old name for a portrait) but also a mind-painting, or even a soul-painting. Though it may be 'a good likeness' it does more than remind you of what the person *looks* like: it makes you understand, perhaps for the first time, what the person *is* like in mind and character. If it is a portrait of a pretty girl who fascinates most of the young men in her circle, the artist, without making her appear less pretty, may have made the portrait tell truths about her that had not been noticed by her admirers – perhaps that she is cold-hearted, selfish, and greedy. It will not be easy, indeed it may be impossible, to discover how the painter has managed to put on to his canvas a picture which is at one and the same time an outside and also an inside portrait. It is unlikely that he will himself know how it was done. If he were asked to explain, he might be able to say no more than 'That is how I see her.'

There are people who dislike going to a doctor because, they say, 'Doctors know too much about their patients!' They feel sure that it is useless to pretend to a doctor. What they may not know is that it is even more useless to pretend to an artist, since few secrets can be hidden from his searching, penetrating, revealing inward eye. Probably no human being has been so mercilessly stripped of the veil of pretence as the outwardly beautiful noblewoman in the famous sixteenth-century portrait (by the Italian painter, Leonardo da Vinci) called *Mona Lisa*, about which an Englishman, Walter Pater, in the nineteenth century wrote almost equally famous words: 'She is older than the rocks among which she sits; like the vampire she has been dead many times, and learned the secrets of the grave. . . . ' As Pater looked at the portrait he was convinced that that lovely face had been a veil behind which lay something very evil.

But we really must hurry back to that cave at Altamira, where we shall find that, even in the Stone Age, it was possible for an artist to suggest more than meets the outward eye.

PAINTING A CAT'S CHARACTER

A painter of animals has fewer opportunities than a painter of men and women for showing more than the outside likenesses of his subjects. Perhaps there are good-natured, faithful, and devoted cows (ask a farmer) and cold-hearted, selfish, and greedy cows; but it seems unlikely that any painter – even William Blake, who once drew the ghost of a flea! – could paint cow-portraits in a way which would make clear to us whether they were cows of good character or not. Nevertheless, particular kinds of animals have their own particular qualities: devotion is ascribed to dogs, independence and spitefulness to cats, courage to lions, silliness to sheep, and so on. In most instances the animal's face plainly suggests the character of its kind: sheep look stupid, lions look fearless, dogs look soulfully and sentimentally devoted; therefore a painter need do little more than a camera can when he is making pictures of such creatures. But it is harder to paint a portrait of a cat, which has a much more complex nature and is very clever at hiding its feelings. Most cats look so furry and comfortable and picturesque and benign that it needs more than ordinary skill in a painter to indicate that that placid ball of purring indolence on your hearth-rug can change in a moment into a spitting fury or into a lofty contemptuous scorner of those who feed and cherish it. Though there are thousands of drawings and paintings of cats, very few do more than remind us that cats are pretty to look at; they hardly ever succeed in telling us anything about the inner nature of the cat. One of the rare exceptions is the tabby in William Hogarth's group portrait *The Graham Children* (Tate Gallery, London – see plate 16).

This cat has obviously just jumped on to the chair on which it is standing upright on its hind legs, its forepaws with unsheathed claws tensed over the rounded edge. Its eyes are alight with untamed desire to reach the bird in the nearby cage; its whiskers are bristling; and we can sense the hardly restrained energy thrilling the body hidden from us by the chair-back. All we can see is the head and neck and forepaws, yet Hogarth succeeds wonderfully well in communicating to us a great deal about that part of cat-nature in which savage appetite has resisted centuries of the softening effects of fireside indulgence. Cats are lovable and flattering domestic pets while it suits them to be so; but when it suits them to be otherwise they can as easily be wild and lonely hunters to whom a surburban flower-bed serves as a jungle for stalking their prey, the birds. So Hogarth, through a picture in which there appears, among much else, the head and front paws of one cat, tells us the truth about cats; and he does this partly by the expression put into the cat's eyes and partly by the quivering expectancy of the slightly-opened mouth. He made little noticeable alteration in the normal proportions of the cat in order to get the effect he wanted. He did not *distort* it.

ARTISTS RE-CREATE

That word in italics in the last sentence is important to everyone who wishes to understand and enjoy paintings and sculpture. In one way or another, for some purpose or other, many of the world's best artists have modified the physical appearances of human beings, animals, and objects when representing them in works of art. Artists are not bound to follow Nature slavishly. They are re-creators, not mere imitators. Few of them are now satisfied with the point of view of the man who said, long ago, 'All art is imitation.' This saying suggests that art is stale and second-hand, which is never true of genuine art. It is better to say 'All art is re-creation.' Some would go further and claim that 'All art is creation.' That claim goes too far, however. Every artist has to make some use of what the Creator of the universe has already made. No artist can create anything that has not already been created; not even Blake could do that. The best that an artist can do is to re-shape in works of art what the Creator has already made; not because he can better the Creator's handiwork, but in order to assist our dull sight and our feeble understanding. An artist interprets the Creator's handiwork to less-gifted mortals. But we cannot see more or understand better by means of art if the artist is always content to copy Nature exactly. When it is necessary for his purpose that he should modify the natural shapes and proportions of the things he is re-presenting in paintings and sculpture he is privileged to do so.

To all such modifications the term 'distortion' is applied. Distortion means 'altering the shape', though most people use it exclusively in the sense of 'making ugly'. Consequently they complain about distortion in modern art, which they think ugly, and do not recognize that distortion is also present in many other works of art which they like very much. Greek sculptors of about 2,500 years ago were especially interested in the physical beauty of men and women, but they had to face the fact that many human beings were not beautiful, even in ancient Greece. However, some Greek thinkers believed that whatever exists on earth is only, at best, an imperfect copy of the perfect pattern existing in the mind of God (though they would have used a different form of words to express their belief). We can easily understand what they meant if we think of something we have ourselves set out to make from a pattern, let us say a model aeroplane, or a woollen jumper. The chances are that when we have finished we know only too well that the pattern we had before us is better than the completed article made by our hands, even though we ourselves may have thought out the pattern in the first place. The perfect thing – the pattern – is created in the mind; the finished object may be very good, but it is extremely unlikely to be in every respect identical with the pattern.

'IDEAL BEAUTY'

If we believe that Creation began when the idea of a perfect universe first shaped itself in the mind of God, and that the universe in which we now live has from various causes become an imperfect reflection of that Divine Idea, we must also believe that men and women have fallen short of the original pattern. That is what the artists of classical Greece believed, though we must not think of them as believing it in the Christian manner. They worked out what they considered to be a perfect physical pattern for their statues of young men and women. That is to say, in the quest of 'ideal beauty' they modified bodily proportions.

Opinions about beauty alter from time to time, and from place to place, and even from person to person; but, right down to the present day, the 'Greek ideal' has been widely accepted in the western world as the highest type of human beauty. Yet it is not the only possible standard, and since the physical proportions of the Greek ideal are an artificial 'improvement' of the common proportions of the human body, it must be said that the Greeks *distorted* for the purpose of 'improvement'. If you still hesitate to agree that this should be called distortion, and you could ask the opinion of, say, a Hottentot (who has his own peculiar ideas of beauty), you would discover that he had a very poor opinion of the Greek ideal form. If you were then to say, 'Well, I'd rather trust the opinion of an ancient Greek than that of a Hottentot!' it would have to be pointed out to you that what we call 'beauty' is largely a matter of where and when one is born and what one has become used to.

WHAT IS BEAUTIFUL?

It is very important to understand at an early stage that *the principle of distortion* in art has played an important part in painting and sculpture from the earliest times. It is particularly noticeable in the art of our own period, and has caused much unfavourable comment from those who (usually unawares) accept and approve distortion in Greek art but reject it in modern art. Greek art, they say, is beautiful, but modern art is ugly. They would be nearer to the mark if they were to say: 'We think Greek art is beautiful because we are used to it. We think modern art is ugly because we haven't had time to get used to it.' While we are free to say that we like the results of one kind of distortion and dislike the results of another kind, we ought not to be in a hurry to declare that one kind is 'right' and another kind 'wrong'; both give a false impression of Nature and therefore both are either equally wrong or equally not wrong.

But, you may ask, cannot anyone help me to know whether a thing is beautiful or not? No. No one can help you to make a *final* decision, because it might so happen that some peculiarity in yourself stops you from seeing beauty in things that many other people agree are beautiful. What you can do, if you are really interested, is to look at things which have been considered beautiful by various people in various places at various times. Among these you will probably find certain types of beauty which appeal to you more than others, though you must be prepared to find that in five or ten years' time another type will appeal to you instead.

Ideas of beauty depend upon age, education, nationality,

social advantages or disadvantages, and physical condition. We should beware of applying the words 'right' and 'wrong' to works of art, lest we run into confusion. Though we need not agree with those who say that art has nothing to do with morality, we can at least keep our heads clear and refrain from joining those who take it for granted that what pleases their own taste is moral and right, and that what does not please them is immoral and wrong. Good people, even if they are saints, are not necessarily good judges of art, though they often pretend to be. They know they are not qualified to instruct a physician about medicine, an engineer about machinery, a judge about law; but art, they seem to think, is anybody's business.

ANGRY NOISES

What is even more curious is that people who rarely go to see paintings they might enjoy will rush to look at those they know they will detest. When an exhibition of Picasso's later pictures was held in London some years ago, immense crowds swarmed to the Victoria and Albert Museum, though comparatively few went to the Constable exhibition which followed it. While struggling to catch a glimpse of Picasso's paintings, one heard such comments as 'All humbug!' 'The man can't even draw!' 'He's only pulling our legs!' 'Ought to be burnt!' The air vibrated with mocking and angry and spiteful and ignorant noises made by ordinarily peaceable men and women whose modesty and good manners and sense of humour had suddenly been driven out of them by a collection of unfamiliar pictures. It is no offence to dislike Picasso's strange and disturbing works, nor to decide that one would not care to have them in one's own home, but no sensible person condemns before he has tried to understand.

Pablo Picasso is a Spanish artist who spent many years in Paris, where he was in contact with numerous other painters who had unorthodox ideas about art. He made many drawings in a straightforward, traditional style, and these are so beautifully done as not only to prove that he is as good a draughtsman as anyone could be but, also, as to persuade us that if he had been satisfied to go on with pictures of that kind he would have become successful and popular among those people who now attack him. After some years had gone by he took to painting in a very different manner. The men and women on his canvases ceased to appear human. Their features became broken up and separated and altogether hideous and horrifying.

We have seen that an artist may live in a world of his own, a world of the imagination in which he sees angels, as Blake did. Even for Blake, however, life was not all angels. He knew that there are devils as well as angels, evil as well as good, darkness as well as light. Yet he was an optimist who looked forward to a time when earth would be transfigured and become very heaven –

> Our souls exult, and London's towers
> Receive the Lamb of God to dwell
> In England's green and pleasant bowers.

Blake lived through the time when Napoleon was a dark shadow over Europe, and while the early effects of the Industrial Revolution were sowing misery among those working under the new factory system. He spoke of 'dark satanic mills', but he could not know of the greater misery that was to come a century later from two world-wars and from the wave of fiendish barbarism which at times threw humanity back to the level of the beasts of prey. If Blake had been living to-day his pictures might have been full of devils.

A NIGHTMARE PAINTING

Now although it will probably be a long time before we can know enough about Picasso to enable us to understand his paintings fully, we shall be less inclined to say stupid things about them if we consider the possibility that he is a very sensitive man (no one who is insensitive can be an artist) who suffers a great deal because of the pain that has been inflicted upon human beings by human beings in his lifetime. Few of us can now believe that angels are dancing beside us, and it should not surprise us when we find Picasso and others painting pictures in which we can find little beauty. In a nightmare world we must expect nightmare art.

Being himself a Spaniard, Picasso could not be indifferent to the civil war in Spain in the 1930s, and during that dreadful struggle he produced one of his most hotly discussed works. He called it *Guernica*. Guernica, a small undefended town in northern Spain, was unforgivably and murderously bombed from the air without warning one day during the civil war, and decent people everywhere were horrified by the wanton slaughter of unoffending children, women, and men. Many painters in the past have produced war pictures, but most of them did little more than show what war *looked* like to someone watching a battle. Very few war pictures give us any notion of what war *feels* like: of the sensations of fear, pain, panic, paralysis, chaos; of an eternity of suffering crammed into a split second. If an artist believes that it is his duty to try to convey to those who think of war as just a misfortune happening to people a long way off (and the Spanish civil war was no more than that to the great majority in other countries) some idea of what war is really like, there is not much purpose in showing bombs exploding, houses collapsing, tanks churning the ground, guns firing: these are only the outward trappings of war, things seen by the eye and heard by the ear. How is a painter to suggest, by means of a picture, what goes on inside the human beings who suffer in war?

Picasso's *Guernica* was an attempt to answer that question. To look at, it is a chaotic mix-up of distorted bodies arranged in a queer rhythmical pattern. If we ask, 'Is that what Guernica, or some part of it, looked like while it was being bombed?' the answer is 'No, of course not.' If we ask, 'Does the picture suggest what it *felt* like to be in Guernica at that moment?' the answer depends upon whether our imagination is lively or dull. *Guernica* may at first seem ugly, and nothing but ugly, to anyone who is not a painter or an art expert. The actual bombing of Guernica was a very ugly affair, and no artist who attempted to prettify it or to be romantic or sentimental about it could easily be forgiven. The purpose of art, it has been said, is to bring order into chaos, and that is what most of us would wish art always to do. It is pleasant and comforting, it may even be ennobling, to look at pictures which are more orderly than life is, to be shown beauty where we are unable to find it for ourselves. But not even art can be wholly beautiful at a time when life itself is often far from beautiful. Truth will out, whether the truth is beautiful or ugly, so we cannot rightly complain when, on occasion, an artist paints an ugly subject.

There is this to add, however: an ugly subject may make a beautiful *painting*. Indeed, if an ugly subject is painted uglily no one will accept it as a work of art.

We were led away again from the Altamira cave-paintings when we began to discuss distortion in art, which took us off to Greece but has led us back to Spain by another route.

FEARFUL YET SPLENDID

Even if conscious distortion did not enter directly into prehistoric painting, those early artists seem to have known by instinct how to get certain effects by emphasizing particular physical features in an animal. The huge beasts in the Altamira paintings are most impressive to us because they communicate the idea of terrifying strength and brute energy. Enough imagination went to the painting of them to make us think not of enormous animals merely, but rather of mighty instruments of irresistible power – living dynamos. We can well imagine that the artist was in deadly fear of them, and through his paintings something of that fear comes across the many centuries which separate us from him. Yet he painted in such a way as to make us certain that, however much afraid, he was also attracted, just as we are attracted by lions and tigers in a zoo, though we should be frightened out of our wits if we met one loose in our own garden.

By what means did the Altamira painter indicate at once the strength and the power of the bison, and also his own human fear and fascination? In Plate 1 you will notice the massive hunched shoulders of the animal, which make us feel that if it were to come to life and rush at us it would be as though a mountain and a tornado had both hit us at the same moment. We should have no chance of escape. When we have looked rather longer at the picture we become less conscious of its fearsome aspect and begin to think of this bison as a splendid creature given a special kind of beauty by the painter. He might have made it frightening and nothing more, but he has, instead, made it majestic and noble. We can see that he gave as much care to this painting as a present-day artist might to a portrait of a Derby winner, or of a Cabinet minister, or of a film star. We take delight, as he must have done, in the lovely sweeping curves where the reds of the shoulders and haunches meet the dark browns of the back and ribs; and by a cunning arrangement of lines and shading we are made aware of the tremendous weight and bulk of the bison, and of its vast rounded shape.

ART IS USEFUL

Why did the Stone Age men make such paintings? Perhaps as an enjoyable pastime during the long nights; perhaps because an irresistible urge to make beautiful things had

already gripped certain men; perhaps as a record of successful hunting; perhaps for some purpose of magic or primitive
religion. A modern author wrote, 'All art is useless.' He
meant that when an artist makes a beautiful work our
enjoyment of its beauty is quite enough to justify its making,
and that we ought not to expect art to have any additional
moral or religious or practical value. But if Early Man had
been mentally capable of argument and discussion, he would
most likely have disagreed entirely with Oscar Wilde's
opinion and replied, 'On the contrary, all art is *useful*.' There
is plenty of evidence that ancient art almost always served
a serious purpose, usually a religious purpose. We must
remember that all the peoples whom Christians call heathen
and pagan had a religion of some kind, a religion which
played a far larger part in their daily lives than Christianity
does in the lives of most English-speaking people nowadays.
They thought it was absolutely essential to exert themselves
in special ceremonies intended to keep their gods in a good
temper, or to conciliate them if they appeared to be angry.
Idols (which are a kind of sculpture and therefore works of
art, however ugly they may appear in our eyes) were either
images of tribal gods or were themselves regarded as gods.
If the idol was treated well, with plenty of offerings and
sacrifices, the god was pleased (so men believed) and would
send a good harvest, or whatever else was needed at the
time.

Primitive religious ritual often took the form of symbolic
imitation – a dance or a play signifying some desired happening – or a painting of the thing desired. The great bison
may have been painted when food was short, in the hope
that the act of making the picture would ensure successful
hunting. Though there is no surviving evidence that the
Altamira and similar paintings had a ritual purpose, the
possibility can never be ruled out from primitive art. It is
likely, however, that these pictures were made simply because someone found that drawing and painting passed the

time very pleasantly and improved the appearance of the cave walls and ceilings. Whatever the motive, there were our forefathers, ten thousand or fifty thousand years ago (opinions differ widely about the dates), decorating the interiors of the places they occupied. And that is what people all over the world have continued to do ever since.

2

What Makes an Artist?

WHEN we walk through an art gallery and hear the remarks made by other people, or look at the faces of the silent ones, we shall probably think that many of them are puzzled by what they see, and that some of them are bored. Only the minority seem to be really enjoying the pictures. The majority are there perhaps because they have been told that they 'ought to go some time', or because it is a wet afternoon, or because they are on a holiday and feel in duty bound to visit all the places of interest mentioned in the guide books, or because they have been led to believe that properly educated and cultured people should 'know about' art.

There is really only one sensible answer we can give if we are asked 'Why do you go to look at paintings?' That one sensible answer is 'Because I enjoy them.' We are compelled to learn a good many things that we do not enjoy, but we are truly educated only by what gives us genuine enjoyment and satisfaction, so long as we understand that lazy people who make no effort get no real enjoyment. Enjoyment is an active state, not a passive one. Nevertheless, it is stupid to suppose that we cannot be educated except when we are learning laboriously and dismally. The best-educated and the happiest men and women are those who enjoy learning and also enjoy their work as much as their play.

It is true that looking at pictures and other works of art is a proper part of education and culture, but it is a waste of time – and a most boring waste of time, too – if we look without some knowledge and understanding of what we are looking at and of what we should be looking for. Most Americans are bored if they are taken to an English cricket match, just as most Englishmen are bored at an American football game. But to the English who understand what is going on, cricket can be the most absorbing and fascinating of all games; while to Americans well versed in its strategy and tactics, their kind of football is a source of excitement and enthusiasm. Knowledge and understanding lead to pleasure and enjoyment.

NEVER TOO OLD FOR ART

Some are fortunate enough to be born with natural abilities and capabilities which others have to acquire by study. There are 'born cricketers' and 'born hockey-players'; there are also 'born artists' and 'born art-lovers'. Those with a natural liking for paintings and sculpture may be able to understand, and therefore to enjoy, works of art without being told what to look for. Many more are born without this gift, however, and need a helping hand if they are not to be cut off from one of life's greatest pleasures.

Let us make no mistake about this: though Art may be 'taught' as a school subject, and though young people may be taken to picture galleries as a part of their education, time so spent is time wasted unless it leads sooner or later to a fuller, richer, and more enjoyable life – to a life which has more genuine fun in it than it would otherwise have. When we are young, looking at paintings and other works of art may seem dull in comparison with playing games, or going to a dance, or joining in some other kind of social amusement; but experience proves that learning to enjoy works of art is a much better mental, spiritual, and even emotional investment. It is a source of pleasure which never leaves us. We grow at length too old to run about, or to dance, or to be thrilled by parties, but we are never too old for works of art, when once we are on good terms with them. Indeed, they give us a kind of enjoyment which increases year by year throughout our lives.

If we discover how to enjoy paintings, not only do we find our pleasure increasing the more we look at them, but we shall almost certainly develop a liking for other things which we should not else consider beautiful or think of as works of art.

HOW DO WE KNOW WHEN SOMETHING IS 'JUST RIGHT'?

It is often hard to find the time or the opportunity to visit an art gallery, but nearly everyone has to move about the streets daily, and in the streets we can see beautiful works of art, if our eyes have been opened. For example, even in streets which (as we sometimes say) have seen better days, there may be delightful wrought-iron balconies and beautiful fanlights, remaining from Georgian (including Regency) times. Iron has now come to be regarded as one of the ugliest of metals; why then should old iron railings on an old balcony ever be thought beautiful? There are at least two possible reasons. First, they can be beautiful because of the pattern into which the iron has been shaped. Secondly, they can be beautiful because the metal has been used in a way and for a purpose which seems exactly right. A beautiful *iron* balcony would not seem equally beautiful if it were imitated in another metal, such as brass or lead, even though the design were copied exactly. On the other hand, we sometimes see beautiful old leaden rain-pipe heads and cisterns which would be ugly if copied in iron.

Why?

That is a somewhat mystifying question.

USING THINGS THE RIGHT WAY

Every material has a quality – a nature – which is peculiar to itself. A particular material gives of its best only when it is used in a particular way and for a particular purpose. We might even say that particular materials are never *happy* unless they are used in the right way for the right purpose at the right time. Iron has a quality – perhaps it would be better to say that it has a *texture* – which gives of its best and seems 'happiest' when it is softened in a forge and then hammered into shape on an anvil by a smith. It is then strong and durable, and the smith's hammer gives it an appearance which looks proper to the material and for the purpose to which it is put.

To forge and hammer iron into shape is, however, slow and expensive. A much quicker and cheaper way is to make a mould of the required shape and to pour molten iron into it. By that means hundreds of *cast-iron* balcony rails can be made in much less time than it takes to make one *wrought-iron* one. As both are made of iron it might be thought that the former is as good as the other; but it seldom is. Cast iron has a different texture and a less pleasing surface than wrought iron; and because cast-iron objects are mass-produced by machinery in a factory, whereas wrought-iron objects are mostly made by hand one by one and each under the control of a single craftsman, the latter seem to absorb from the man who made them something personal which comes from the interest he took in the job he was doing.

A boy who carves a stick from a branch he has cut for himself puts something of himself into it: it is, in a special sense, *his* stick. It may not be as straight and smooth as a stick bought in a shop. The knots may not be all neatly planed away, as they would be if the stick passed through a machine in a stick-making factory. If the boy tried to sell the stick he would very likely be told 'I can buy a better one for half the price.' But *would* it be better? The boy probably wouldn't think so. Nor ought he to think so. While he was shaping the stick, probably with his pocket knife, he became for the time being a *craftsman*, and a craftsman is a person who takes pleasure in making things, not merely a person who makes things because he gets paid for them. If, in addition to whittling and shaping the stick, the boy had seen in his mind's-eye some pattern or design that he wanted to carve in the wood, he would then be more than a craftsman: he would be an artist also.

ARTISTS MUST ALSO BE CRAFTSMEN

What has been called the 'mind's-eye' of the boy might better be called his imagination. It is a bold and risky thing to lay down a hard and fast definition of an artist, because not everyone will agree with any definition that can be given. We shall not go far wrong, however, if we say that *an artist is a person who creates in his imagination* and that *a craftsman is one who makes with his hands*. Yet we must go farther than that. We all create in our imagination, and thus far we are all artists of a sort. Any one of us may be, like the poet Gray's villager, a 'mute inglorious Milton'. Any one of us may be a creator of invisible masterpieces of painting. But we cannot claim to be artists unless we are able to make apparent to other people what we have created in imagination. A person who imagines a poem is not a poet unless he can put what he imagines into proper shape in either spoken or written words. A person who makes up a tune 'in his head' is not a composer unless he is able to sing it aloud or write it down for others to sing or play. A person who has pictures in his mind is not a painter unless he also has the skill to show what is there by making the pictures visible in paint on a canvas or some other surface.

'. . . *Unless he has the skill.* . . .' What it really comes to, then, is that *an artist is one who has both the ability to imagine and the skill to present in visible or audible form*, whereas a craftsman need not have more than the skill to carry out what someone else has imagined for him. The smith who makes the beautiful balcony railings may have had a design drawn on paper for him by another person. If so, the smith is a craftsman only. But if he himself created the design also, is he then an artist? Certainly he is, though there might be disagreement about this, because a distinction is usually made between the 'fine arts' and the 'applied arts'. This is a pity, since it has led many people to believe that the Fine Arts (usually spelt with capital initials to suggest that they are superior to the applied arts!) are more important because they are assumed to be for decoration rather than for use.

FINE ARTS AND APPLIED ARTS

Chief among the recognized fine arts are painting, sculpture, and architecture (as well as poetry and music); among the applied arts are pottery, furniture, weaving, embroidery, and so on. In recent times the distinction between the two has been breaking down, and most people would now be inclined to agree that what matters is not the label but the quality and merit as well as the beauty of the article or object. A painting is not necessarily a work of fine art. If it is a good painting, it is; if it is a mediocre or a bad painting, it is not. A beautiful jug ought not to be put automatically in a lower class simply because it is to be used for the practical purposes of a jug. Even if we were to say that the term 'fine art' should include only those things which are so beautiful that no one will dare to use them for fear of damage or destruction, that would at once appear absurd when we recollect that a beautiful house – however exquisite it may be as a specimen of the fine art of architecture – exists to be lived in, i.e. to be *used*.

The reason for dwelling here upon the difference, or lack of difference, between the fine arts and the applied (i.e. useful) arts is that we shall go completely wrong if we think of any branch of art, however fine, as useless. A beautiful painting is useful as an object to live with. It is true that we are not able to live, in the physical sense, with the master-pieces of painting which hang in public art galleries. But a lover of pictures can live with the great masterpieces all his life if he takes them into his own memory. We can memorize a painting by exercising our visual memory, just as we can memorize a poem by exercising our verbal memory. We only need to remember shapes and colours and spacing, instead of words. If you are one of those people who enjoy singing while they bath, you will find it a pleasant change sometimes to lie back quietly and 'see' on the bathroom ceiling the great paintings you remember with your inward eye.

You may ask: 'Isn't it better to buy some coloured post-cards of the paintings I like? I shall remember them more easily by that means.' Certainly it does no harm to buy these and look at them often. And as there are many great paintings that most of us will never have the chance of seeing in galleries abroad, we must be content to look at printed reproductions of them. It is all the more necessary, there-fore, that we should know thoroughly well in the first place what a painting is.

ENJOYING PAINTING

There are, of course, many different kinds of paintings, and many different ways of painting, and many different sub-jects for painters. But there is one thing present in every painting, whatever its subject, its kind, its manner. That one thing is PAINT. Such an elementary and obvious statement may well have made you curl your lip in contempt as you read it. It is none the less a fact that paint is the last thing most people notice when they look at a painting. A good many lookers-at-paintings never notice the paint at all. If you ask them what it is they like about a favourite painting, they may say 'The subject', or 'The colours', or 'Oh, it's so life-like!' But how often have you heard, 'What I enjoy in that picture is the *paint*'? Have you *ever* heard anyone say that? Yet the truth of the matter is that unless we are ready and able to enjoy the paint in a painting we are without the master-key to the whole matter.

Before we go further, it will be helpful to point out that a principal reason why coloured prints of paintings are only a makeshift for the real thing is that there is no paint on them, but only ink. Leaving aside the difficulty of exactly matching the colours of the original by any inexpensive printing process, we must realize that ink is an entirely different substance from paint, different in 'body', in texture, and in 'feel'. These differences are made more evident by the fact that although very few pictures are painted on paper, paper is used for nearly all printed reproductions. If we are to get a correct impression of the original from a coloured print, we need to be able to translate, by memory, the appearance of ink and paper into the appearance of paint and canvas, paint and wood, paint and plaster, or whatever other material was used in the first place by the artist. Paper and ink usually give a smooth and more or less shiny surface. Most paintings also appear to have a flat shiny surface, but there is actually some degree of unevenness and 'ridgyness' in the great majority, because layers of paint are placed one upon another. When the artist uses very thin liquid colours this unevenness is barely noticeable to the naked eye, but there is another kind of painting in which the surface is broken by paint applied heavily as a thick paste. A passage – we use the word 'passage' about a small portion of a picture in the same sense that we use it about a part of a piece of music or of the text of a book – a passage of thick paint affects the spectator's eyes differently from a passage of thin paint, as a *fortissimo* passage in music affects the ear differently from a *pianissimo* passage. Light-waves in the one instance are modified as are sound-waves in the other. These variations in the paint-layers are much minimized, and often obliterated, by the camera lens when the original painting is photographed for the purpose of making the blocks used in printing inexpensive reproductions. So, however useful such reproductions may be for certain purposes – most of us get pleasure from them and are glad to have them – they are not a wholly satisfactory substitute for the real thing, except in so far as memory or imagination enables us to recreate them in terms of the original materials.

DELICIOUSLY MESSY STUFF

All painting is a kind of playing-about with paint, fostered by an elementary passion which many of us begin to indulge almost as soon as we can hold a brush. In infancy we do not love paint chiefly because of what we can draw with it. We love it because it is deliciously messy bright stuff which we can slap and push and splash about. If there were enough of it we should be as eager to make paint-pies as mud-pies and sand-castles. We get what we learn later to call 'a sensuous pleasure' from dealing with it.

In the first chapter we saw that an artist retains in later life more of the unspoiled qualities of childhood than the average person does. The artist's feeling for paint is one of the primary instincts that he has succeeded in retaining. As he gets older he is able to control and civilize that instinct without losing it, so that he usually comes to think more of what paint can be made to do than of what paint is in itself. Usually; but not always. Such a painter as Van Gogh (see pages 156–61), a nineteenth-century Dutchman who was at intervals more than a little mad and therefore much like a child in certain respects, almost wallowed in paint. It is thick on the surface of many of his pictures. Some of them seem almost to be moulded and modelled in paint, rather than merely painted. Whatever we may think of them as works of beauty when we first see them, they leave us in little doubt as to the kind of man Van Gogh was. As soon as we look at his later paintings (the earlier ones were more 'ordinary'), whether they are of fields, or of jars of flowers, or of men and women, or of pieces of furniture, the thick and often swirling paint makes us feel, even though we may have known nothing beforehand of his life and character, that Van Gogh was tempestuous, troubled, and tormented, with a spirit that burned in him as the sun burns in his pictures, drenching them with fierce light and vivid colour. Paintings can be cool and quietening – those of the seventeenth-century Dutch landscape painters, Ruisdael and others, are so – but Van Gogh's seldom are. His are often disturbing, and the disturbing effect is usually produced more by the way he used the actual substance of paint than by the subjects he chose.

THIN OR THICK?

If we watch an artist at work on an oil-painting we usually find that he applies the paint with brushes (having first mixed the colours on his palette), moving the brush with a light stroking motion which lays a thin film, or *glaze*, of colour on the picture surface, and often laying one glaze over another. There are other painters who prefer to put on heavy dabs of paint with a palette-knife instead of a brush. Occasionally they even smear it on with the thumb. When glazes are applied, the thin layers of oil-paint allow the underlying colour to show through to some extent, and this gives a rich glowing quality to the finished picture. No medium other than oil gives such richness and depth of tone. When the paint is applied thickly (the *impasto* method) in a paste-like form as 'pure', i.e. unblended, colour it is opaque and ridgy on the surface. No light is reflected through the paint-layer, but to some extent the uneven surface of the actual paint reflects light at varying angles. Paint may also be applied in very small dots or blobs or dashes of pure unmixed colours placed closely side by side. This method was used by the French Impressionists in the late nineteenth century, as we shall see in Chapter 8.

THE PAINTER SHOWS HIMSELF

There are almost as many ways of painting pictures as there are artists to paint them, for every good painter brings something entirely and exclusively personal into his work. This is not to say that there are a thousand and one ways of using paint, but that a single method used by a number of different painters will produce varying results. These variations and differences from one man's work to another's are what we refer to when speaking of an artist's *style*. We all know quite well that if two girls each wear a frock of the same material and cut to the same pattern, one may look smart and attractive – 'as though she has just stepped out of a band-box' – while the other may look frumpy and dowdy – 'as though she has just been tipped out of a rag-bag'. Style in dress is a quality that belongs less to the clothes than to the person who wears them. And so it is with style in art. A painter's style is his personality showing in his pictures. The styles of Hogarth, Reynolds, and Gainsborough as portrait-painters are all different, and would have been so even if they had all used precisely the same methods of painting. Hogarth was a different sort of man from Reynolds, and Gainsborough was a different sort of man from either of the other two. Therefore they looked for different qualities or characteristics in the people they painted. Therefore their portraits are different in style. Hogarth's style was bluff and vigorous, and he preferred to paint middle-class people and working people. He did some very fine heads of his own servants. Gainsborough's style was more delicate and better suited to the well-born and wealthy people who flocked to him to be painted. Both Hogarth and Gainsborough were, however, fresh and original. Reynolds was a more thoroughly trained and a more learned painter than either of the others (though he did not overcome certain technical weaknesses), but in acquiring immense knowledge he sacrificed spontaneity and originality.

Reynolds did not think it was enough to rely upon personal genius. He believed that every painter ought to try to profit to the utmost from study of the works of all the great artists who have gone before. Painters who believe this are often very clever and accomplished, and Reynolds's accomplishment came near to the highest kind of genius. But there is some lack of freshness in him which makes us feel that he knew too much and felt too little. It is possible that Hogarth and Gainsborough were not such good painters as Reynolds; yet it is possible that they were better artists, if we accept the definition that an artist is one who creates in his imagination before he attempts to make with his hands. The greatest artists are undoubtedly those who convince us that they have seen the world and the people in it as no one ever saw them before.

PAINTERS AND PAINT

We have found that a factor of very great importance in a painting is paint; not only for the elementary reason that without paint there could be no paintings, but because paint is by its own nature a pleasant substance which a painter enjoys using and which we as spectators ought to enjoy as a vital part of his pictures.

We have found, too, that paint can be used variously in painting: thinly as a transparent glaze; thickly as an opaque paste. There are a good many other points relating to methods of painting that we may discover as we get more and more interested in looking at pictures. The effect of a finished painting depends very much upon the method and manner of applying the colours.

We have also found that the use of the same methods by more than one painter will not result in similar pictures, but that each painter brings to his work some personal quality. This may be due to his training and thinking, as in Reynolds, or to his own free imagination and fresh outlook upon life.

Let us now go back to a phrase we have used above: 'paint is by its own nature a pleasant substance'; and to a sentence on page 32: 'Every material has a quality – a nature – which is peculiar to itself.' No one is likely to dispute that a painter, just as all other human beings, has a character which is his own and different from that of anyone else; and that therefore his paintings, if he is a good painter and not merely an imitator, will be unique. But is it reasonable to go farther and claim that inanimate substances such as paint, or iron, or lead, also have a nature of their own which insists on its own rights?

BEAUTY AND USE

Recent artists and art-critics have popularized the phrase (applied more especially to architecture) 'fitness for purpose', which means that a thing – particularly a building, though it is equally true of a teapot, or a fountain pen, or a statue, or anything else – can only be truly beautiful through and through if it not only looks beautiful but also does its job properly. A house may look beautiful outside, but is it completely and satisfyingly beautiful if it cannot be lived in conveniently and comfortably? If it is draughty, if the rooms are dark and stuffy, if the kitchen is wrongly situated or so poky that it is difficult to work in it, the housewife will say that it is not a beautiful house; that it is pretending to be something it is not, and that the person who designed it was a bad architect. A teapot, however lovely to look at, is a fake if it will not pour without dribbling. If a statue, intended to stand in a public place, is made of material which will not withstand local weather conditions, the sculptor has bungled, and no bungled job can be said to be truly beautiful. It would be vain for him to plead that his statue would have lasted for centuries if it had been kept indoors, for he was engaged to make an *outdoor* statue. The statue he made did not possess the quality of fitness for its purpose. The sculptor used the wrong material, or else carved his material in the wrong way.

In these several instances, however, the failure was of a

practical kind. There is another aspect of fitness for purpose which is purely artistic ('purely aesthetic' is a more precise term, but a little more difficult to understand, though it can be looked up in the dictionary). It was suggested on page 32 that though wrought iron is right and fit for balcony railings, lead is not; an old lead cistern looks right, but an old iron tank does not; a wooden farmyard gate looks right, a concrete gate does not; a china teacup looks right, a metal one does not.

AN ENDLESS ARGUMENT

It might be argued that in certain instances the material which does not look right is, for one reason or another, more 'practical' than the material which does; and we might agree that that is so, without being convinced that the 'practical' material has been used for a job suited to its own nature. We would claim that our stubborn opinion is based upon aesthetic sensibility – or sensitiveness to what is right from the artistic point of view – but our opponents would still insist that we are swayed by romantic or sentimental prejudice. The argument might go on until doomsday without agreement being reached, because it rarely happens that practical men know enough about art, or artists enough about practical matters, to enable them to understand one another. Aesthetic sensibility and practical sense ought not to be at loggerheads, yet under modern conditions they are hard to reconcile.

Since the Industrial Revolution, art has been cut off from daily life, though – now that schools are taking more interest in the arts and manufacturers are more ready to agree that there is no need to make a thing ugly merely because it is cheap – there is reason for hoping that art and life will come together again. In the great ages of art in Italy and elsewhere artists were not a class apart. Painters did not paint on the off-chance that some rich man might see their paintings at an exhibition and buy one or two. They painted pictures that were wanted for a set purpose – to decorate a church, a civic building, or a palace or mansion. They painted to order, but they also painted as well as they knew how. The great artists usually managed to satisfy their patrons (some failed to do so), but they did not kotow to them. Patrons had good taste and knowledge of art more often than rich buyers of pictures have nowadays; artists were more often workmen working in a workshop alongside a lot of other men similarly occupied.

Now that men rich enough to be patrons of art are becoming fewer and fewer, at least in Europe, it may be that art will have to be kept alive by the State. Not everyone likes that prospect, for many people sincerely believe that art is so intensely personal that no government department would be able to handle artists widely. But the more we all, as citizens, get to know about art the better it will be for our own enjoyment, even if artists do not become State-employed, i.e. employed by *us* through our elected representatives. If they were to become so employed, the artists' wages would have to be paid out of the rates and taxes, and we should all become art-patrons. We should then want to see that we were getting honest value for our money. But we shouldn't know whether we were or not unless we have some knowledge of art and also, and more important, good taste and good sense.

THE RIGHT KIND OF PAINT

The problem of 'fitness for purpose' has a bearing on the pure enjoyment of paintings.

There are subjects for which only a particular kind of paint appears right; and each particular kind of paint calls for a particular kind of treatment. Certain subjects are suited to water-colours – river scenes, for example; certain other subjects to fresco, to tempera, to pastels (see below and on page 152); and so on. There is a kind of treatment – a special technique – which makes water-colours 'look right'. Certain things can be done in oils which cannot fitly be done in water-colours, and the closer a water-colour painting gets to an oil-painting in appearance the less successful it is likely to seem *as a water-colour*. It is right for an oil-painting to look rich and sumptuous; it is unsuitable for a water-colour to attempt to do so. Water-colours have definite limitations because, of their own nature, they lack 'body', though some painters have sought to overcome those limitations and to give them an appearance of solidity. The most attractive water-colour paintings are those which have a free-flowing and (in the best sense) 'washy' effect, since they are done with what are in fact colour-washes and not with a juicily substantial paint such as oil-paint is.

A large and monumental manner is suitable for frescoes, which are painted direct on to wet plaster walls with colours mixed in water. Tempera – in which the pigments are moistened with yolk of egg – does not allow of graduated shading and is therefore suited to straightforward subjects, simple designs, and formal treatment. One of the characteristics of a good painting is that its style and subject are in harmony with the nature of the medium used by the artist. It makes no pretence to be something it is not.

3

Painters Who Worked for the Church

WE saw in Chapter 1 that the prehistoric cave-painters produced very fine pictures of animals. It is impossible to discover at what date Early Man turned to the painting of human beings. A great deal of his work must have perished long ago, and its story is known to us only in fragments. Scholars have tried to build up that story from the few specimens of cave-paintings so far discovered.

We cannot suppose that the pictures found in the caves at Altamira and elsewhere in Spain and in France are near to the beginnings of painting. There must have been many earlier and cruder efforts which have either finally disappeared or are still to be discovered. What is strange is that Early Man seems to have learned to draw and paint animals cleverly and brilliantly long before he was able to deal successfully with pictures of humans. The earliest specimens we have of the latter (again in caves) are rather like the pictures which very young children make when they begin to draw – blobs for heads and bodies, and matchsticky arms and legs – a kind of pictorial shorthand. But in at least one way these prehistoric drawings are quite different from a modern child's attempts. They often represent hunters in action, and as we look at them we feel how alive and vigorous they are, however little they may resemble the actual physical shape of men. They are not good likenesses, but they are very exciting, and they stir in us the sensations of running and leaping, or whatever other movements are shown. (See Plates 1 and 2.)

It is important that we should notice and think about that particular point, because it has a close bearing upon certain much later kinds of painting. We may be inclined to take it for granted that the prehistoric artists who drew men in

46

what appears to us to be a crude fashion couldn't do any better. That may be so, but we cannot be sure. Throughout the history of art, from the earliest times to the present day, we find painters aiming at one or other of two altogether different purposes: either (1) to imitate the outside appearances of people and things; or (2) to stir in the spectator certain feelings or sensations. The greatest artists are able to fulfil both these purposes simultaneously. Michelangelo (1475–1564), for example, does so. His paintings of men and women on the ceiling of the Sistine Chapel in Rome look remarkably like actual men and women. They also convey to us a sensation of the brooding vision of the prophets, of the wisdom and mystery of the sibyls (or prophetesses), of Adam drawing life from the finger of God. Now Michelangelo was working in Italy in the sixteenth century, when the Dark Ages in which the barbarians had ravaged Europe were long past, and the Middle Ages when the Church became all-powerful were receding. The Modern World, in which Man came to regard himself as the centre of the universe, had been born and was undermining the teachings of the Church. Michelangelo was employed by the Pope, and the paintings carried out by the artist were intended to serve a religious end. But in that period the Popes themselves had become powerful princes, loving splendour for its own sake, though splendour in the decoration of churches might be justified by claiming that it is an aid to worship and an offering to God.

MEN AND GOD

Michelangelo's Sistine Chapel paintings were at once a sumptuous decoration and a glorification of the beauty and strength and wisdom of men and women made in the image of God and not far removed, themselves, from the divine. His Adam is so splendid a figure as to seem part demi-god, part hero, rather than a creature 'born to sorrow as the sparks fly upward'. Far from stressing, as earlier painters had done, man's need of God, Michelangelo makes us conscious, rather, of Man's worldly pride. Though it was bolder in Michelangelo than in other painters, this tendency to glorify Man is a leading motive in the art of modern times, as it had been also in the art of the ancient world of Greece and Rome. But in between the passing of ancient times and the coming of modern times – that is to say, in the Middle Ages – a quite different spirit ruled.

After the Roman Emperor Constantine made Christianity the official State religion in A.D. 324 and shifted the capital of his Empire to Constantinople (A.D. 330), ancient pagan art was submerged by Christian art. Constantinople, previously named Byzantium, became a main centre of the new art, and the style which developed from it and spread far and wide is therefore known as 'Byzantine'. There has been a revival of interest in this East Christian art during the present century, and references are now made frequently to 'the Byzantine style'.

SPIRITUAL PICTURES

The finest Byzantine pictures were not paintings at all, but mosaics in the great Christian churches, among the most famous being those at Ravenna (Italy) and Palermo (Sicily). Since mosaics are made by embedding minute squares of coloured stone and glass in cement, it is almost impossible for the artist to get smooth-flowing curves; he must be satisfied with a somewhat stiff and angular picture. This did not much disturb the Byzantine mosaicists for they were stern religious people who, though they made many beautiful works, did not love beauty for its own sake. They wished most to serve and praise God through their art. Their subjects were nearly always taken from the Bible and the lives of the saints, and even when they were not working in mosaic it suited their strictly religious outlook to produce pictures which were rigid and awe-inspiring, not human and tender; pictures which led the spectators' thoughts away from the things of the flesh to the things of the spirit.

We should keep in mind that these men, until the time of Constantine, had found it a painful experience to be Christians. Persecution had bred in them a dark outlook upon the world, just as concentration camps have done in many people to-day. Religion was to them, as politics are to many now, an inescapable duty, whatever pain and misery might befall them. Holiness, saintliness, profited the spirit but chastened the body and brought physical suffering and privation.

If we remember this it should help us to understand why the Byzantine artists so often introduced into their pictures – into paintings as well as mosaics – gaunt figures that look disproportionately tall and thin. Religion does not welcome new ideas and new fashions, and once the Byzantine style for Christian art was established it persisted for a thousand years. It was replaced in southern and western Europe only when the capture of Constantinople by the Turks in 1453 sent the scholars of the Eastern Empire fleeing westward, leaving Byzantine culture still in possession in Russia and parts of the Near East. In those regions, even as late as the seventeenth century, paintings were being done in a manner almost identical with that of the eleventh century and earlier. The Byzantine style, in fact, has a continuous history in Russian art and has survived all political and social upheavals.

THREE DIMENSIONS IN TWO

There is another important aspect of Byzantine pictures which we have not yet mentioned. Not only is it harder to get curves than angles in mosaics, it is also difficult to get light and shade, without which it is almost impossible to suggest depth in a picture, or to produce what is called a 'three-dimensional' effect.

Actually, a picture has only two dimensions: length (or height) and breadth (or width). When a painter wishes to indicate depth he has to make use of a technical device or convention – a 'trick of the trade' as it were. We know that as we look into the distance along a street, horizontal parallel lines appear to slope and run together to a 'vanishing point'; while solid objects appear less dense the farther they are away. Anyone walking along Fleet Street towards St Paul's Cathedral in London and looking up Ludgate Hill will notice that the cathedral dome looks almost semi-transparent in the morning light, while the nearby buildings remain solid-looking. So in order to get the optical illusion of depth (the third dimension) an artist makes the going-away lines slope towards each other: that is, he uses the device of *linear perspective*. He also modifies his colours in order to indicate the apparent decrease of density in distant objects: that is, he uses the device of *aerial perspective*. Furthermore, by the use of graduated shading he is able to suggest the bulkiness of solid objects: this is called *modelling*, a word borrowed from sculpture.

In mosaics it is easy enough to get linear perspective; aerial perspective is less easy; and modelling is still less easy. But the Byzantines were not interested in such matters, whether they were mosaicists or painters. They were not 'realists'. They did not want to imitate the world they saw round about them, for that would have distracted their attention from the sacred themes connected with the spiritual world. Early Byzantine paintings are 'flat' in appearance. The objects in them look as though they were cut from sheet metal or some other thin opaque material; there is no suggestion of roundness or solidity, and the saints and holy people in them seem to have plenty of soul but little flesh and blood.

When the Byzantine influence spread westward into European centres of Christendom, into Italy particularly, its chill harshness became gradually warmed and softened.

But the degree to which its spirituality became humanized varied from place to place, even in Italy. (Plates 3 and 4 show something of the stiffness which early Italian and early English painting inherited from Byzantine sources.)

A TOWN ON A HILL

The little Italian town of Siena, in Tuscany, had many trading contacts with the East and, standing as it did on a hilltop, it was slow to feel the gentler and more worldly atmosphere that was developing elsewhere in Italy. Towards the end of the thirteenth century Siena became one of the most important Italian art centres. About the same time Florence, not very far away, was also beginning to produce great painters, and many priceless masterpieces were to come from both places. But whereas the Florentines were a vigorous go-ahead people, scientifically minded, eager to experiment and to acquire knowledge, the Sienese were quiet, sedate, orthodox, and unprogressive. In Florence, therefore, the Byzantine spirit from abroad was soon absorbed and transformed into something new and strange and wonderful. In Siena, on the contrary, it lingered and saturated the local paintings with a good deal of its own special character.

However much the manner of painting changed in Florence and other European cities as the new outlook on life became widespread, the majority of pictures continued to deal with religious subjects until after the sixteenth century. Though many painters of Christian pictures seem to have been what we should now regard as unreligious men, the Church remained for many generations the principal art-patron. Painters, whatever their opinions and beliefs, would therefore have been hard put to it to make a living if they had been unwilling to decorate the walls and ceilings of churches and monastic buildings. Usually – not always – we can judge what kind of man a painter was by 'the balance of interest' displayed in his pictures. That is to

51

say, when in a Madonna and Child the artist appears to have got most enjoyment from painting the dresses, or the background, or in bringing in other figures not essential to the main subject, it is likely that if he had been free to choose his subjects he would not have painted religious pictures at all. We shall find that in Florence and Venice the Church called to order certain artists whose interest in painting for painting's sake, or in other worldly matters, led them to soft-pedal the religious note in their pictures.

HEAVEN AND THE WORLD

The Sienese painters, however, were not tempted to run any such risk. Even though their earliest great painter, Duccio, was a turbulent fellow, he managed to keep at least one eye steadfastly upon the Christian purpose which his works were required to serve. Beautiful though his pictures are, Duccio did not move very far from the stiff formalism and religious severity of the old Byzantine manner. He does not suggest to us, as the Florentines and others were to do later, that however desirable it may be to get to the other world of heaven, there are many lovely things to enjoy in this present world in the meantime. It is true that in his *Madonna in Majesty* (Siena Cathedral Museum) the Virgin is seated on a magnificent throne, but almost the whole of the background is filled by the haloed heads of saints and angels, and the Holy Mother is holding her Child with more reverence than affection.

In these early Italian paintings it was customary to place the sacred figures against a flat gilded background, which gives splendour to the picture without distracting attention from its Christian purpose. Duccio's *The Three Marys at the Tomb* (see Plate 5) – painted on the back of the *Madonna in Majesty* (the whole work was an altar-piece for the cathedral in Siena) – has this gilded background, but between it and the angel and the three women are mountainous rocks. This is an early instance of the introduction of landscape into a religious painting, though 'landscape' is not perhaps an appropriate word here, if we think of a landscape only as a picture of a pleasant stretch of country in which we should like to walk. Duccio's towering rocks do not lure our eyes or mind away from the women and the angel and the empty tomb; rather do they emphasize the solemnity of the scene. We can also discover a further purpose in those rocks.

ARRANGING A PICTURE

If we enjoy a painting at all, a part – it may be a large part – of our enjoyment comes from the *composition*, even though we may not be aware of it. 'Composition' is, briefly, the *arrangement* – positioning, spacing, proportioning, and relationship – of the figures and/or objects and colours which make up the whole *design* of a painting. There may be only one point or there may be many points of interest in a picture, but however many there are they must be *unified*, i.e. brought together by some means into a single harmonious relationship. If while we are looking at a picture we find our eyes wandering about, up and down and here and there, it is likely that it is the work of a clumsy artist. The moment we glance at a painting, our eyes should be led to a particular part of it – the *focus*, or *point of rest*, or whatever term we choose. We must, of course, recognize that if we, as spectators, are inattentive, or stupid, or antagonistic, we may defeat the artist's intention. We must co-operate intelligently with the artist. No one can lead us by hand or eye unless we are willing. So if we get nothing from a painting the fault may be ours; but it is reasonable to expect – and it may even be promised – that if we are sensible and receptive a good painting will have something worth-while to give us.

In Duccio's *Three Marys* our eyes are led immediately to

the angel's face. He is not at the centre of the picture, but a
little to the right of centre. The women are at the extreme
left, and as there are three of them to only one angel, it
might be supposed that our eyes would be drawn first in
their direction. Why is it that they are not? It is not that the
angel is an outstandingly splendid figure. He wears light
draperies; the women's coloured robes are more immediately noticeable. All have ornamented golden haloes. The
angel's face is the visual point of rest in Duccio's painting,
because the composition of the picture is based upon (*a*) an
upright rectangular mass formed on the left by the three
women grouped together and weighted down, as it were,
by the almost flat-topped hill rising above their joined
haloes; (*b*) a larger triangular mass which becomes visible
at the shoulder of the innermost woman. This triangle
formed by the mountain is repeated in the smaller triangular
arrangement of the angel's figure and wings and robes as he
sits on the raised lid of the tomb. Our eyes tend naturally to
rise to the apex of a triangle, and as the angel's face is at the
apex of the lighter triangle framed in the larger and darker
triangle of the mountain, it is to that point that our eyes are
led as soon as we look at the painting. Further, the eyes of
all three women are turned to the angel's face and our eyes
follow theirs. 'But,' someone might ask, 'the angel is looking
at the three women, so why shouldn't our eyes follow his and
make the women seem more prominent than he?' The
answer is that the three pairs of eyes influence us more than
the other pair.

It will be found that there is an underlying geometrical
design (based on cube, pyramid, cylinder, spiral, or some
variation or combination of these) in many paintings, but
the basic pattern is often much more difficult to trace than
it is in the present one. We might more properly have described the main part of the composition in *The Three Marys*
as pyramidal rather than triangular, for although Duccio
retains even here some Byzantine formalism in the woman's

figures and draperies and in the general severity of the composition, he has not followed the old medieval flat two-dimensional manner. His picture has depth, though far less depth than it would most probably have had if it had been the work of a Florentine painter, and less than we find in Sassetta, another Sienese, whose landscape backgrounds are delightful.

TOO MANY GOOD THINGS

If we were asked to express in the fewest words possible the distinguishing features of Sienese painting, we could hardly do better than say that it is simple, reverent, and tender in feeling, and restrained in style. These qualities are displayed charmingly in Francesco di Giorgio's *St Dorothy and the Heavenly Child* and in the central figure in Matteo di Giovanni's *The Madonna of the Girdle* (both in the National Gallery, London). In the former, few traces of the old Byzantine frigidity remain, and the child Christ has become a little Italian boy dressed in a 'pale cream-red smock over a blue dress and lavender stockings', and carrying a miniature basket of roses and apples. *The Madonna of the Girdle* is an elaborate composition, with a numerous angelic choir and musicians, and a heavenly audience. But it is more interesting in its parts than as a whole. If that is a fair comment, it means that the artist has failed to *unify* his composition. We ought not to be able to say of any painting, 'This bit is more interesting than that bit.' *The Madonna of the Girdle* could be divided up to make about thirty attractive pictures, several of them completely enchanting, but as a single picture it seems over-populated with good things which, taken all together, do not add up to a single whole. Though it is not at all suitable to apply an arithmetical formula to works of art, it may help to make this particular point clear if we say that the parts of a painting ought to seem to add up to exactly 100 per cent. If we feel that the total is, say, 87 or, as in the case of *The Madonna of the Girdle*, much over 100, something is wrong either with the painting or with our appreciation of it. Nevertheless, in Matteo di Giovanni's picture, the head and shoulders and hands of the Virgin, with her sunburst halo and with blue angels peeping over her shoulders, are in themselves wonderfully satisfying. The demure innocence of expression, the prayerful hands, the liquidity of the veil, the rose-red dress, the embroidered white robe, give the kind of enjoyment which brings a smile of deep pleasure and a sigh of content.

PAINTING PEOPLE'S FEELINGS

The paintings referred to so far, in this chapter, have been of saintly and sacred subjects and far removed from the kind of people and the kind of emotions familiar to most moderns. We have not yet come to the stage where artists took to painting portraits of actual people simply as portraits and without disguising them as biblical characters or saints. That could not come about until there were wealthy men able to compete with the Church in employing artists to make pictures for them, nor until artists had become used to the idea of producing paintings to express something other than religious sentiment and piety.

Among the Florentines, one of the first to strike an entirely new note was Masaccio, in the early part of the fifteenth century. In his most famous picture, *The Expulsion of Adam and Eve from Eden*, painted in the Brancacci Chapel of the Church of the Carmine in Florence, he not only made a striking advance by showing fully-rounded, solid-looking human beings standing free from any flat conventional background, he also conveys powerfully to the spectator that the sinning outcasts are feeling pangs of shame and remorse such as most people know, however mildly, at some time in their lives. Adam and Eve's despair comes less from dread of the angel with the sword who hovers menacingly over them than from the terror and horror in their own breasts, which memory will never allow them to banish. And it is Eve that this searing pain torments the more agonizingly in Masaccio's painting. Here we have, then, the beginnings of *individual characterization* in art, that is, the attempt to show that different people feel differently, and to indicate the effect of those different feelings or different intensities of feeling.

But though, for modern minds, Masaccio is in certain respects the most interesting Florentine painter of his time, it was Giotto who paved the way, a century earlier, for the new style in painting; and he also had a forerunner – Cimabue. Giotto did not free himself altogether from the Byzantine manner, but he did something the Byzantines had rarely done: he used his own eyes and tried to paint what he actually saw. The typical Byzantines, as we have already noted, turned their eyes from the life of the world round about them and had no wish to paint creatures of flesh and blood. Giotto was not an impatient revolutionary. He kept his artistic impulses under strict discipline, and although he brought a strong current of fresh air into an incense-laden and almost stifling atmosphere, many of his figures seem still to be half-held in a devotional trance. Art had been, for centuries, like the Sleeping Princess; now the kiss of awakening was given, but the cramped limbs needed time for the blood to flow strongly in the veins again, for the muscles to loosen into free movement, and for the stiffened garments to become pliable. Giotto's magnificent frescoes in the Arena Chapel at Padua and Santa Croce in Florence show that art was coming back to life, but their mood is still one of serene solemnity.

This might also be said to be the keynote of Fra Angelico's work. In fact and in spirit he was a cloistered monk whose vision was confined by monastery walls and by a life utterly dedicated to religion, though there is feminine sensibility in Angelico, contrasting with Giotto's masculine severity. Angelico's best-known picture, *The Annunciation* (see Plate 6), part of a series of frescoes he was set to carry out in the Dominican convent of San Marco in Florence, is one of the simplest and most straightforward masterpieces in the world. The Virgin sits with crossed wrists on an arched veranda, inclining in humility to the genuflecting Angel of the Annunciation, whose multi-coloured wings emphasize by contrast the simplicity of form and colour which gives to the picture a dignity that is beyond the power of words to describe. A plain board fence divides the enclosed garden from the woodland outside, and on the veranda (or loggia) the discreetly carved capitals (the tops) of the columns relieve the otherwise bare architectural setting. The Virgin's face shows only humility. This picture belongs to a spiritual dream-world, noiseless, passionless, sinless, unapproachable except through a lifetime of cloistered virtue. (See also page 103.)

A RUNAWAY

What seemed to Fra Angelico an ideal existence was unbearable to the Carmelite monk Fra Lippo Lippi, the orphaned son of a butcher. He was sent to a monastery in boyhood and fretted against the life ever after. We know his story well through Robert Browning's poem, *Fra Lippo Lippi*, which tells of his escapades and of his impatience with the kind of painting he was required to do. The poet imagines the painter-monk describing how he has been rebuked for putting too much beauty and not enough religion into his pictures. He is told:

> Make them forget there's such a thing as flesh.
> Your business is to paint the souls of men –
> Man's soul, and it's a fire, smoke . . . no, it's not . . .
> It's vapour done up like a new-born babe –
> (In that shape when you die it leaves your mouth)
> It's . . . well, what matters talking, it's the soul!
> Give us no more of body than shows soul!

Here's Giotto, with his Saint a-praising God,
That sets us praising, – why not stop with him?
Why put all thought of praise out of our head
With wonder at lines, colours, and what not?
Paint the soul, never mind the legs and arms!
Rub all out, try at it a second time. . . .

The painter replies:

   Now, is this sense, I ask?
A fine way to paint soul, by painting body
So ill, the eye can't stop there, must go further
And can't fare worse! . . .
Why can't a painter lift each foot in turn,
Left foot and right foot, go a double step,
Make his flesh liker and his soul more like,
Both in their order? Take the prettiest face,
The Prior's niece . . . patron-saint – is it so pretty
You can't discover if it means hope, fear,
Sorrow or joy? won't beauty go with these?
Suppose I've made her eyes all right and blue,
Can't I take breath and try to add life's flash,
And then add soul and heighten them threefold?
Or say there's beauty with no soul at all –
(I never saw it – put the case the same –)
If you get simple beauty and nought else,
You get about the best thing God invents:
That's somewhat: and you'll find the soul you have missed,
Within yourself, when you return him thanks. . . .

In Fra Lippo Lippi's *Virgin Adoring the Child* (Berlin Museum) religious painting has escaped from Christian sobriety as lightheartedly as the painter himself played truant from the monastery when the call of the outside world became too strong. The infant Jesus, looking like a well-rounded cherub and with his finger in his mouth, lies naked in a flower-strewn wooded and rocky landscape. The

Madonna, a young girl such as Fra Lippo himself no doubt knew and admired, kneels beside the Child, enveloped in a robe of beautiful soft blue. The Heavenly Father looks down, His hands outstretched above the holy white dove from whose breast shine golden rays descending upon the Child. The young St John stands on a rock path to the left, intent on something out beyond the front of the picture which has captured the whole of his attention, making him just a mischievous boy, not an apprentice saint. A bearded old man in a white habit kneels in prayer higher up the path. The wood has a theatrically romantic appearance which makes us think more of Merlin and other story-book magicians than of the Holy Family. This is a beautiful picture, but one in which Fra Lippo Lippi's eager love of the world and humanity carried him near the brink of sentimentality. He escaped from the harsh discipline of the monastery cell, and Browning's poem persuades us to give him our sympathy; but he would have painted better pictures if he had learned the self-discipline which enables an artist to keep his emotions from running away with him.

4

Beginning to Enjoy Pictures

LIFE is too short to allow us to read all the good books or all the good paintings. For it is not enough to glance at paintings, nor is it enough merely to look at them; they must be *read* if we are to get lasting enjoyment from them.

While we are infants we are taught the alphabet before we can begin to read, then we progress from simple books to more difficult and complex ones. That is the common-sense way, and it would seem reasonable to set about beginning to enjoy pictures in a similar fashion, starting with what is easy and working upward. So in infants' schools we often find pictures which are supposed to be the sort that babies ought to begin with. Usually they are large, brightly-coloured prints of animals and children playing or doing nothing in particular. It is a pity that often they are not good as pictures: sometimes they are mawkish, or senti-mental, or even downright silly. Of course pictures meant for infants' eyes should be simple, but they should also be first-class, and there is no reason at all why good coloured reproductions of some of the world's masterpieces should not be hung in nurseries and schoolrooms so that babies can see them. If a child did its lessons, or played, or went to bed in a room where, say, Fra Angelico's *Annunciation* (see pp. 57–8) was hanging, it would be likely to take as much in-terest in that as in a picture of a kitten patting a ball of wool. Though the child would not at first know what Fra Angelico's picture is 'about', its lovely shapes and colours would be attractive. When we say that it is best to start with simple pictures we need not use the word 'simple' in the sense in which it is used of printed matter. A 'simple' book is one in which there are few long words and no complicated thoughts;

61

a 'simple' picture is one in which the design and colour-scheme are straightforward, not one which tells a 'simple' (i.e. a naïve) story.

Most of the engravings and presentation plates from Christmas magazines which so often decorated the walls of Victorian parlours told a simple story, but they were usually crowded and confused, commonplace in design, and crude in colour. Because they have been introduced to none but poor and unsuitable ones in childhood, many people grow up to expect little more from pictures than that they should be 'pretty' in colour and 'nice' in subject. But how boring life would be if we could say no more of our brothers and sisters or of our best friends than 'She is a pretty girl' and 'He is a nice boy'. We need more than the surface qualities of prettiness and niceness; we need beauty and character, qualities which have depth and permanence. Whether in people or in pictures, simplicity can go hand in hand with beauty and character. So even if we are only beginning to take our first hesitant and halting steps among paintings, we need not be timid about going straight into the company of the masters, both the Old Masters and the newer ones.

A LITTLE AT A TIME

But let us come back to the difficulty mentioned in the opening sentence of this chapter – that life is too short to enable us to get on familiar terms with all the good paintings.

There are in the National Gallery in London round about five thousand paintings. If we spent half an hour on each picture it would take us nearly fifty weeks, six days each week and eight hours each day, to get from one end of the collection to the other! You may say, 'Surely no one need spend anything like half an hour on every picture!' Obviously no one could, unless he made the National Gallery his full-time occupation for the best part of a whole year. And then he would still have the Tate Gallery, the Victoria and Albert Museum, the British Museum, and other important public collections of paintings to inspect, in London alone. Yet half an hour is very little time to give to getting to know a work to which the artist may have given a fair slice of his life; and certainly no good painting will yield up its beauty and character to anyone who is not prepared to allot sufficient time to it.

What, then, are we to do?

In the first place we must realize that the quickest way to kill any chance of enjoyment in an art gallery is to put in too much time at any one visit. Our feet soon get unbearably tired, and many people quickly find themselves suffering from a 'gallery headache', which may be caused by eye-strain or by an over-dose of mental concentration. We cannot enjoy paintings, or indeed anything else, unless we are physically at ease. Some enthusiasts say that the best plan when visiting an art gallery is to 'do' one room at a time. That isn't bad advice; nor very good advice either. We should have to ask which room we are to 'do' first. Should we begin in the room with the latest pictures, or in the one with the earliest?

If we were to go straight to the modern paintings, we should find ourselves having to bother with various problems – of subject, of style, of treatment, and so on – which would be easier to deal with if we already knew something about the earlier painters' works. We should, in effect, have got to the roof without knowing enough about what supports it underneath.

On the other hand, if we began with medieval paintings we should probably find them monotonous, whereas if we had known beforehand what they led up to they wouldn't have struck us in that way at all. Nor would there be much point in starting with one of the middle rooms, for that would be rather like starting a book at page 100 without reading what went before.

Of course, anyone who sets out with a grim determination to be 'a serious student of art' may find it useful to work out plans and time-tables and all the rest of it, and to do the whole thing in a grimly determined way. But he will miss a lot of fun. If the aim is to *enjoy* the paintings, the best plan at first is to have no plan. Most of us find that a love of books and reading comes from browsing among books in early years, not by setting out to read solidly through literature from Homer to Bernard Shaw. Planning is something that comes later, when love of reading has produced a steady enthusiasm and staying-power. So it is with art. Start by browsing among pictures.

LITTLE BY LITTLE

Go into the nearest art gallery and walk through the rooms fairly quickly, stopping only before those pictures that 'hit you in the eye' and pull you up. Those will be the ones that really have something to say to you at that moment. As soon as you begin to feel tired, turn round and walk out into the open air again.

When you get home it is possible that you will say, disappointedly, 'I saw only one picture that I really liked.' The sensible answer to that would be, 'Good!' If, however, you were to say 'I saw fifty pictures I liked', the sensible answer would be, 'Bad!' For it would mean either that you weren't honest with yourself and pretended to like what you thought you ought to like, or that you had detected very little difference between the various kinds of pictures.

The poet who wrote 'We needs must love the highest when we see it' was writing nonsense. Most of us do nothing of the kind. We may come to love the highest after we have first spent a good deal of time looking at it without understanding, or even with distaste. If, in rare instances, we do love the highest as soon as we see it, we seldom love it because we *know* it is the highest. Be chary of saying 'I *love* such-and-such a painting' when you mean no more than 'I *like*. . . . ' When you have known a painting for ten years or so and have looked at it a hundred times with the eye of knowledge and understanding, you may claim to love it; but if you were carried away by hasty enthusiasm, you may after ten years be saying 'I can't think what I ever saw in that picture to make me say I loved it!' Such changes of opinion need not disappoint us. They may be a healthy sign of development. We *grow into* respect and love of things and people we were at first indifferent to or disliked. We also *grow out of* earlier enthusiasms, because we develop and leave them behind. This is not to say that it is right for us to be in a constant state of chopping and changing and blowing hot and cold throughout our lives. There must be a permanent core of interest and devotion and principle to keep us on a steady course; but we can no more expect to wear the same mental and emotional clothing from youth to maturity and on to old age than we can expect or wish to wear the same suit or the same frock.

OUR TASTES CHANGE UNTIL . . .

So if you find, later on, that the paintings which caught your attention most on your first visit to the art gallery have taken a lower place, you will no doubt find also that you now enjoy others that you then passed by. At length you will have sorted out and settled your opinions and formed your taste. You will have found a regular circle of friends among the paintings.

But we are running too far ahead.

That first excursion in an art gallery should be followed at intervals by others, until you have been through all the rooms. By then you should have discovered the *kind* of paintings you like best and can make a real start from there.

If you felt most at home in, let us say, the Flemish room, you will want to know who the Flemish painters were, when they lived, where they worked, why they painted in that particular way, and so on. Having seen some of their pictures and enjoyed them you can read about them more intelligently and with more interest than if you had read about them beforehand.

Or you may have preferred the landscape paintings. If you did, you can concentrate on those at later visits, finding that landscape gradually came in as a background in early Italian religious paintings; that it grew to occupy more and more of the picture-space; that at length the figures became subordinate to the landscape setting; that, later still, there were landscapes with no figures; that some landscape paintings are notable for cloud effects, some for atmosphere, some for the beautiful treatment of river scenes; some because the artists were fascinated by scientific problems of light and colour. There are scores of byways to explore.

Or you may have taken a special liking to the works of one painter. You will then want to know about his life and training; about other painters who influenced him; and about later ones who were influenced in turn by him.

A STARTING POINT

The important thing is to start from something that has genuinely interested *you*. Then you will go along under your own steam and find enough to fill your leisure pleasantly for the rest of your life. All that is needed to set you going is that you should find, out of the thousands, at least one painting which excites you. The rest of the story will develop as fast as you may wish it to, though unless you have an abnormal appetite for art you are unlikely ever to find that you can enjoy all the great paintings equally well. You may find yourself indifferent to, or even disliking, paintings that everyone else says are wonderful. Give them – and yourself – a fair chance of getting on good terms, but if the result is still negative, never mind. Either you have a blind spot (each of us has, somewhere) or your nature is not in harmony with that of the painter. We can't nag ourselves into liking what we are not ready for. We must have patience with ourselves and not be in too much of a hurry. But, at the same time, we have to learn that ignorance and prejudice are nothing to be proud of.

There will be a further stage for you to travel. Having taken a general view of some period or kind of painting or of some particular painter's work and followed the various side-tracks into which you will find yourself enticed, you will be ready not only to look at pictures but also to read them in detail. This will give you much more enjoyment. There is as much difference between reading a picture and merely looking at it as there is between really tasting food and merely swallowing it.

'SCHOOLS' OF PAINTING

Gallery catalogues and books on art use such terms as 'Italian School' (of which 'Florentine School', 'Venetian School', etc. are sub-divisions), 'Flemish School', 'Spanish School', 'English School', and so on. Though to say that a painter belongs to such-and-such a 'School' usually means that he was born in that particular country or region, it sometimes means that he worked there though he may have been born somewhere else. In other instances it means that the artist painted in a manner similar to that of other painters working in a particular locality. Thus, Holbein is described as belonging to the German School both because he was born in Germany and because he painted in the German style, though he worked in England for considerable periods, became Court painter to Henry VIII, and made an extensive series of beautiful tinted drawings of Tudor ladies and gentlemen. El Greco, on the other hand, is catalogued as of the Spanish School, although he was born in Crete and worked in Italy before he settled in Spain where he painted his greatest pictures in a manner partly Byzantine, partly Spanish, but mainly El-Grecoish (if we may invent an ugly term) for he was one of the most original of all painters. Whistler was born in America, went to Russia with his family, back to America, then to France to study in Paris, to England, to South America, to Venice, and back to London, where he died after having done most of his best paintings there. His style owes something to Spanish art, something to French, and much to Japanese, but almost nothing to English. Yet Whistler is labelled 'British School'. So it might appear from this that such labels mean very little. To say that a painter belongs to the Italian School is extremely vague, because so many different styles of painting have been practised in Italy, but it does nevertheless help us to recognize and memorize the special qualities of a painter's style if we learn that he is of the Sienese School, or of the Florentine, the Venetian, Roman, Umbrian, or some other Italian regional School.

THE PAINTER'S 'STYLE'

From the fourteenth to the eighteenth century certain groups of Italian painters congregated in particular centres and painted in a manner peculiar to each centre. Of course, as time went on, the manner in any one locality might change: there is at first a period of fading-in, as it were; then what we might call a full-development period; then, finally, a fading-out. Sometimes a painter would move from place to place, changing his manner to resemble that customary in the new centre in which he settled for a while. Even so, most painters had a favourite manner of their own, as the greatest painters always have, apart from any local manner they may adopt. It is this distinctive personal style which enables their work to be recognized even when no signature appears. Thus, although Botticelli and Michelangelo are both described as of the Florentine School, there is no possibility of mistaking the pictures of the one for those of the other. Botticelli had none of the full-blooded vigour and flamboyance of Michelangelo; there is an exquisite but rather finicking delicacy about the former (and occasionally a touch of sly humour, as in the National Gallery *Mars and Venus* where the little fauns are playing tricks with the lance and helmet of the sleeping warrior-god), while the latter is bold and monumental. We can imagine Michelangelo roaring with laughter if he were amused, but Botticelli would probably have been moved to nothing more than a quiet smile, and it is not at all surprising to know that he became a devoted follower in Florence of the fanatical preacher Savonarola. Nor is it surprising that Michelangelo went to carry out his greatest works amid the papal splendours of Rome.

LIFE-LIKE PAINTINGS

If, then, it could include two painters so very different as these, what common factor was there in the Florentine School? In contrast to Sienese painting which, as we have seen, was for the most part devoutly religious, Florentine painting had a strongly scientific leaning. It is true that in Florence religious pictures still far outnumbered all others, but, unlike the Sienese, the Florentines were less concerned with Christianity than with the craftsmanship and technical problems of painting. They were determined to make their pictures as life-like – as much like the people and things in the world they actually knew – as they possibly could. The more difficult a problem of painting was, the more enthusiastically they set about solving it. Flat backgrounds were abandoned, and in their place came vistas and distant prospects of country scenes which called for great skill in the use of perspective, as can be seen in Antonio Pollaiuolo's *Martyrdom of St Sebastian* (National Gallery, London) where the landscape background includes a wide view of the valley of the River Arno with the city of Florence far off in the distance.

Another Florentine, Leonardo da Vinci, though one of the very greatest of all painters, was more interested in engineering than in art, and he brought into his paintings that intense love of experiment which is as precious as life itself to men of a scientific cast of mind. This was not always good for Leonardo's pictures, for he ruined his masterpiece, *The Last Supper*, painted on the refectory wall of Santa Maria delle Grazie, Milan, because he insisted on using what appears to have been oil paint laid on a plaster surface, instead of the method which time and experience had proved best for fresco painting – namely water-colours which would bind chemically with wet plaster and become permanent. Yet even if he had lived to see the picture as it became, flaking and peeling and faded, he probably would have had little regret. He had tried out his experiment and it had failed, but he would have argued that without experiment there can be no progress. That represented the true Florentine spirit, and in the total of its varied achievements the Florentine School has never been surpassed.

The Umbrian School, to which Perugino and Raphael belonged, is much admired for the mellow warmth of atmosphere and colouring which is its outstanding feature. It produced many lovely paintings, but they seem drowsy and listless like an autumn afternoon in comparison with the Florentines' which are fresh and stimulating like a spring morning.

SHOWING OFF

The Roman School (which must not be confused with the art of ancient Rome) favoured a somewhat violent manner in which there are startling melodramatic contrasts of vivid light and sooty shadow. In Caravaggio's paintings, the most typical of the Roman School, the artist seems to be not an honest experimenter working in the true scientific spirit, as the Florentines did, but a self-conscious performer concerned mainly with posturing and showing off his own cleverness. This rather theatrical mood was to lead to the *Baroque* style which spread across Europe in the seventeenth century, chiefly in architecture and sculpture, but to some extent in painting also. Baroque art was dominated by a passion for suggesting movement: in sculpture and painting, by figures in rhythmical contortionist attitudes and often in intertwining and towering groups; in architecture, by elaborate masses of ornament and twisted columns. It is magnificent and often richly beautiful, but sometimes overpowering, and occasionally ridiculous in its utter want of restraint.

Those who love gorgeous brilliance may claim that the Venetian School was greater than the Florentine, though there is no good reason to declare that either is superior to the other. They are the twin peaks of Italian painting – twins in their stature only, not in their character.

A map helps to show why Venetian painting differed so much from that of Florence and other Italian regions, for art is much affected by both geography and politics, which are themselves usually inseparable. We know very well that British political, social, and industrial history has been controlled by Britain's position as an island looking to the Old World on the one side and to the New World on the other, and for long protected from foreign invasion by the surrounding seas. The coming of swift means of communication and transport has now made geographical situation less important; but in the fifteenth century, when the great age of Venetian painting began, the position of the city – a seaport facing east and with water-ways and marshy ground hampering its dealings with the mainland – placed Venice in the strange position of being more nearly oriental than Italian. It sent its ships and merchants to the East, imported sumptuous materials from the East, and fell under the spell of Eastern colour and splendour. Venice became a rich and

71

independent state, aloof from the strife between warring rival princes which afflicted Florence and other Italian cities. It was also less dominated by the papal authority of Rome.

FLORENCE AND VENICE

Florence, almost at the centre of the land-mass of Italy, stood open to the torments of civil war, which, as always happens, produced an atmosphere encouraging such spiritual and moral puritanism as were expressed in the preaching of Savonarola, the poetry of Dante, and the paintings of Giotto, Fra Angelico, and others. The Florentine concern with science and engineering was to some extent due to wars and the need to invent machines for military defence and attack. While others were fighting, Venice was trading; and the commercial and civic prosperity she enjoyed are reflected in Venetian painting – in the splendour of colours (what could surpass the sheer, almost insolent, richness of Venetian red?), the well-nourished bodies of the people, the costly furs and fabrics, the feastings and processions, the luxurious buildings and assemblies. The art of human portraiture, of which other Italian cities had produced fine examples, was in Venice carried on by Bellini and Titian to a new level of excellence; while the latter's swirling and golden-toned *Bacchus and Ariadne* (National Gallery, London) gives expression to an undisguised pagan joy of life. Even when a Venetian artist preferred cooler colours, as Veronese did, there is no lessening of splendour. It was Veronese who was summoned before the Inquisition because his *Feast in the House of Levi* (Accademia, Venice), commissioned for the decoration of a monastery, gave more space to a clamouring horde of publicans and sinners and merry-makers than to the central group at the table with Christ. The great triple-arched apartment at the head of a double balustraded staircase belongs to a palace of royal proportions and affords a perspective, through the arches, of other palaces in the space beyond. Here in this painting is the spectacle of wealth and worldly pride triumphant. Veronese excused himself for introducing 'fools, drunken Germans, dwarfs, and other oddities' by simply remarking that he had certain spaces to fill, and therefore adorned them with figures of his own invention.

Venice was at length brought down by the inward decay which is a result of too much prosperity, and it was already a degenerate city before Napoleon's conquering shadow fell upon it. Happily, two eighteenth-century artists, Canaletto and Guardi, painted many views of Venice, and of its festivals and ceremonies, before its real life came to an end. These were, however, relatively sombre painters, more inclined to topographic accuracy than to the exercise of personal imagination. The last vestiges of the dying splendour of Venetian painting are seen in Tiepolo's work; but, though something of the old proud manner lingers there, the spirit has gone. A mechanical artificiality took the place of the former genuine joy of life, and Tiepolo's theatrical mannerisms became merged in the Baroque when that, too, was in decline.

ART WENT TO CHURCH

The Italian painters were so numerous – nearly 250 are represented in the National Gallery (London), divided among fourteen 'Schools' – that the 'Italian style' is in fact a group of regional styles, each congregated around a local nucleus, not a single national style. Italy itself, of course, did not become one united nation until long after its amazing fruitfulness in the arts was exhausted. Although it may not account for everything, the patronage of the Church was largely responsible for the unparalleled wealth of Italian masterpieces in architecture, sculpture, and painting. There were hundreds of sacred buildings to put up and to decorate. Art became a habit, an admirable and excellent habit, and where the Church led, the secular princes and nobles followed. The original demand for religious paintings in Italy can be traced in part to the climate of the country. The brilliant sunlight caused churches to be built with comparatively small windows and comparatively large areas of wall space which required decoration and therefore provided much work for painters.

TAKING PAINS

In the northern Catholic countries of Europe, where Gothic architecture flourished, churches had very large windows and, consequently, limited wall-space. Stained glass therefore largely took the place of wall-paintings for church decoration. Religious pictures continued to be used as altarpieces however, and the Flemish and German painters produced noble masterpieces in that form (e.g. the Ghent altarpiece, *Adoration of the Lamb*, by Hubert or Jan van Eyck), while in Flanders and France, particularly, the decoration of psalters and other religious books fostered a great tradition of miniature-painting for the illumination of manuscripts. It is in fact to such small-scale paintings that special features of the Flemish School can be traced. The illumination of manuscripts does not often call for outstanding imaginative gifts in the artists who practise it. It calls, rather, for extreme care and close attention to detail in the execution of the work. These were qualities in which the Flemings excelled. Imagination may tend to run riot in southern climates, but in the north people are more matter-of-fact, and northern artists are more inclined to paint what they actually see with the physical eye than what they might with more effort see with the mind's eye. But no hard-and-fast rule can be laid down. One of the greatest Flemish artists, Rubens, after a stay in Venice, returned to his own country to paint with a quite un-Flemish exuberance and amplitude; though, even then, he preferred to keep as close as he could to actuality, employing his wife as model in picture after picture, as the Madonna and as Mary Magdalene, as well as in pagan subjects and in straightforward portraits.

A PICTURE FULL OF THINGS

For work more typically Flemish we can turn to Jan van Eyck. Few paintings by him are now known, but those few are masterly. *Jan Arnolfini and his Wife* (Plate 9) shows all his qualities at their best: his skill in painting life-like portraits which accept plainness of countenance as a fact to be recorded honestly, not falsified into comeliness; his power of marshalling numerous objects and details, painting them with loving care and the utmost realism, yet keeping them subordinate to the unified design of the picture. A man, a woman, a dog, two pairs of pattens, a chandelier, a lighted candle, a mirror with a scene reflected in its convex surface, ten miniatures set around the mirror-frame, a tasselled rosary hanging from a nail (even the nail has its full share of the painter's care and attention), a brush, a chair, a cushion, a rug, a board floor, a four-poster bed, a window, a chest, four oranges; for the man – a black hat, a black under-gown, a fur robe, stockinged feet; for the woman – a white linen, lace-edged head-dress, a voluminous green robe edged with fur over a blue dress and exquisitely ornamented in a minute pleated pattern below the fur on the hanging sleeves. Each and every one of the objects and details is a source of prolonged pleasure, and the closest scrutiny reveals no flaw in the craftsmanship. Each different substance – fur, cloth, linen, wood, glass, metal, enamel, fibre, hair, flesh, orange-skin – is exactly rendered. Yet (this is the point that needs to be emphasized in regard to this picture) notwithstanding his delight in detail-painting, Jan van Eyck has given us first and foremost a completely unified composition, a superb masterpiece. We are never allowed to neglect the main intention of the work: it is a portrait of a man and his

wife. The *point of rest* is the face of the woman. Her figure is
in full light, the man's in shadow. Both figures are cone-like,
their clothes being widespread at their feet, and our eyes are
led upwards to the faces; to the woman's most definitely,
since her face is the most brightly lit section, and further
emphasis is given to it by the white head-dress which begins
at her forehead and reaches to her shoulders. The face is
therefore not only strongly lit from the front but is also
framed in light.

PAINTINGS AND PHOTOGRAPHS

Other Flemish painters were particularly happy in painting
diaphanous fabrics, showing their semi-transparency and
their every crease and fold and curve. If they introduced a
gilt filigree buckle every thread of the intricate design was
painted with absolute fidelity. Such concentration on detail
might be dismissed slightingly as mere photographic realism,
but as this was long before the camera was invented, painters
were then required to do the kind of work the camera can be
used for now. But there is more than that to say. No photograph can persuade us that the camera enjoyed making the
picture. When a photographer is a master of his craft and
not merely a person who pushes a button or presses a bulb,
a photograph can have a living quality. The pictures taken
by Fox Talbot and Julia Cameron during the early years of
photography, in the nineteenth century, have that quality.
Nearly always, however, a photograph is obviously a
machine-made object.

'Never anything can be amiss when simpleness and duty
tender it,' says Theseus in *A Midsummer Night's Dream*. It is
because the Flemish painters give us the feeling that simpleness and duty – and the love of doing a job supremely well –
governed whatever they put their hands and eyes to, that
we get deep pleasure from their painstaking art and find it
lastingly enjoyable.

5

Paintings of Everyday People and Things

So far, in this book, we have been doing what the beginner was advised in the previous chapter to do on first visiting an art gallery. We have been browsing among pictures: lingering over a few which at once attracted and interested us, talking haphazardly about subjects and styles and methods and processes and developments, but taking no notice whatever of a hundred and one things that we should need to study if we set out to follow the progress of painting from prehistoric times down to the present.

Yet we have noticed at least one particular line of development in European painting between about the eleventh century and the seventeenth – namely, the slow but steady change of emphasis from heavenly personages to earthly persons, and from flat gold and other plain backgrounds to elaborate landscape settings.

In early Byzantine paintings the Virgin and Child and other saintly figures were made to look more than human, or at least different from human; but in Italian and in Flemish and French paintings the Madonna and Child are, quite evidently, portraits of Italian, Flemish, or French young mothers with babies also of local birth; while the setting in which they are placed is local too, not the Holy Land.

A WAY ROUND

So although in one respect painting became more naturalistic and people and things were made to appear as they actually were within the painter's knowledge, artists at that time saw nothing odd in taking biblical history out of its Eastern surroundings and transporting it to Europe for pictorial convenience. We should now think it very odd indeed if an English artist were to paint a *Madonna and Child* in which a Cockney girl and her baby were placed in a scene showing the Thames and the Houses of Parliament. Such a picture could be defended, however, on the plea that it might make the story of Jesus and his Mother seem more real to modern Londoners than if the artist painted a Palestinian woman and child against a view of Bethlehem. If the Italian and other painters worked out any theory at all in this matter, it no doubt was that the people worshipping in the churches where their paintings were to be seen would be more impressed by homely pictures than by foreign-looking ones, or even by supernatural-looking ones. What is much more probable is that most of the artists *wanted* to paint local people and local scenery, and that the only chance they had of doing so in those days was by putting such persons and places into pictures with religious titles. In some instances when a rich man employed an artist to paint a sacred picture which he intended to present to a church, an undisguised portrait of the donor would be put in the foreground, usually as a kneeling figure doing homage.

RICH MERCHANTS AND POOR PAINTERS

We see, then, that on one pretext or another the growing interest in humanity and this present world took a firm grip on the art of painting even while the Church still held spiritual control in Europe. After the Reformation, in those northern countries which freed themselves from allegiance to Rome, secular paintings began to outnumber religious ones. The conditions for this change were especially favourable in Holland, where a stubbornly Protestant people with abundant commercial prosperity and strong civic pride, but no liking for ornate churches, encouraged painters of non-religious pictures. Merchants bought pictures for their houses; town guilds and corporations, taking pride in themselves as citizens working in the public service, were pleased to hang pictures of themselves and their colleagues in town halls and other official buildings. These gentlemen, however, were neither connoisseurs of art nor generous patrons. They wanted the pictures they ordered to be good likenesses, and they were not willing to pay large sums of money for them. Consequently the Dutch painters were often poor, sometimes very poor. If they failed to produce the kind of pictures expected by their hard-headed and tight-fisted employers, they would find themselves cold-shouldered and with their paintings left on their hands. It would have been useless for any one of them to say, 'I am a genius, so I must be allowed to paint the kind of picture I want to paint.' The burghers' answer would have been, 'If you paint the kind of picture *we* want, we will pay you for it. If not, we shall have nothing to do with it, or with you.'

BEAUTY DISCOVERED

Living in such circumstances, the greatest of the Dutch painters, Rembrandt, found himself unpopular and neglected. But he was a great man as well as a great artist, and nothing could keep his genius in check nor discourage him from painting masterpieces, whether anyone wanted them or not. When no other subject was at hand, he painted portraits of himself. That turned out to be very fortunate, because those self-portraits by Rembrandt are among his finest works, and they enable us to judge what he was like at various ages. As he was not only a genius in the art and craft of painting, but also a man who couldn't help throwing light on the inward character of those whose portraits he painted, we can learn from the self-portraits how Rembrandt aged in body and also how, in the face of an unfriendly world, he grew in wisdom and serenity of spirit as the years went by. He was almost certainly the world's greatest painter of elderly people, both of old men and old women. It is true that, as Browning makes Fra Lippo Lippi say,

> If you get simple beauty and nought else,
> You get about the best thing God invents

– but, to repeat what has already been stressed, it is an error to suppose that beauty and prettiness are one and the same thing, or that when a face ceases to be pretty or handsome, after youth has passed, no beauty can remain. Walter de la Mare has written

> But beauty vanishes; beauty passes;

in his *Epitaph* on a lady of the West Country, yet his own poem disproves it. The lady's beauty lives on in the poem and also, no doubt, in her gracious influence on those who knew her. An artist, whether poet or painter, is a preserver of beauty which *would* otherwise vanish; he is also a discoverer of beauty where others might not find it. Rembrandt was both discoverer and preserver. Behind the wrinkled countenances of the old people whose portraits he painted he discovers beauty of character for us, and thus transforms what we might otherwise dismiss as ugliness. In *Macbeth* Duncan says

> There's no art
> To find the mind's construction in the face.

Duncan, however, was not an artist, or he would have known better. A good portrait-painter has the power to find the mind's construction in the face, and it was his exceptional power in this respect that makes Rembrandt's portraits so great.

LIGHT AND SHADE

Another remarkable feature in Rembrandt's pictures is his intensely dramatic use of chiaroscuro (i.e. light and shade).

As was mentioned in the preceding chapter, the Italian painters belonging to the Roman School used masses of light and dark in a crude and violent fashion. It was left for Rembrandt to show the most effective way of handling that kind of picture.

In addition to being one of the greatest painters, Rembrandt was also the greatest of all etchers and dry-point engravers. (An *etching* is a print from a drawing made in reverse on a copper plate treated with acid-proof varnish. The lines drawn by the artist with a needle scratch through the varnish, so that when the plate is put into an acid bath the uncovered metal is eaten away and the design bitten permanently into the plate. When it is inked and wiped, the ink stays only in the hollows etched by the acid. Paper pressed on to the plate picks up the ink, and the scratched design appears as a picture embossed on the paper. A *dry-point* is similar to an etching in appearance, but the design is cut direct into the metal plate with a harder metal point, and no acid is required, though sometimes a picture is a combination of etching and dry-point.) Etchers and dry-point engravers can, if they wish, work over their designs on the metal several times, taking prints at the various stages: these are called 'first state', 'second state', and so on. In the British Museum Print Room are a number of Rembrandt's etchings and dry-points in their several 'states', and from these we can see how he improved them.

This brief digression on a subject outside the scope of this book is introduced here because the importance of chiaroscuro in Rembrandt's works can be seen clearly if the earlier states are compared with the final state of his dry-point called *The Three Crosses*. In the earlier states, light is fairly evenly distributed over the whole surface of the picture, whereas in the final state the centre is brilliantly lit and the surrounding portions heavily shadowed. We have only to compare the last with the others in order to recognize the immense gain in force and dramatic interest which comes from Rembrandt's brilliant use of contrasting lights and darks. He was too resourceful an artist to employ this device tiresomely often, but how striking it can be in a painting is shown by *The Young Warrior* (see Plate 12), in which the powerful effect of the light gleaming on the armour and helmet would be lost but for the deep surrounding shadow.

PLEASING ORDINARY PEOPLE

Rembrandt died in loneliness and poverty, but it should not be thought that because *he* was unable to paint his masterpieces in a manner that satisfied the taste of his time, the other seventeenth-century Dutch painters were no more than artisans carrying out their masters' orders. Most probably Rembrandt would have been a misfit in any country at any period. However much we venerate his memory and stand awed by his great power, the world could not go on if such men as he were not very rare. Their influence is too disturbing and explosive for a workaday world. This does not mean that supreme genius is always at loggerheads with the hum-drum little men. Shakespeare had not much liking for what he called 'the groundlings', yet without flattering them he managed to write plays which were both popular and profound. The general run of Elizabethan London theatre-goers who went to Shakespeare's plays enjoyed the blood and thunder of *Hamlet*, but few of them would have puzzled their heads about the problems of Hamlet's character which scholars have discussed learnedly and solemnly in so many books that they would now fill a library.

Similarly, most seventeenth-century Dutch painters, Rembrandt excepted, managed to satisfy the public taste of their age without lowering their own artistic standards – if they were conscious of possessing anything so impressive. It is more probable that they liked the same subjects as ordinary people then liked, and that what chiefly interested them was not *what* to paint but *how* to paint. How tiresome all those 'Dutch interiors' would be if they were not painted so delightfully.

THE 'FEELING' OF THINGS

Few artists have put into their pictures a more commonplace collection of objects than those in Vermeer's. Yet Vermeer is ranked among the great painters – because he had a marvellous eye and a wonderful hand: a marvellous eye for knowing how common objects could be made a hundred times more interesting by being arranged and spaced and lighted in a certain way; a marvellous hand for translating into paint not simply the appearances of things but also their 'feel', i.e. their texture and their weight. This is an ability shared by other Dutch painters of the period, though Vermeer surpassed them all in this special gift, and he also had the secret of painting in a manner which gave his pictures a smooth enamel-like finish. He not only painted the effects of indoor (and occasionally outdoor) light with amazing skill, but he somehow makes it seem as though cool light is coming from the picture itself. The word 'cool' is important here, because Vermeer did not use light in Rembrandt's dramatic – and sometimes tragic – manner by throwing either a bright beam or a rich glow into the midst of deep shadow. Vermeer spread across the picture a gentle light which, in his interior scenes, comes through a window on the left side. He offers us serenity, not excitement – except the quiet simmering excitement which is aroused in many of us when we are in the presence of perfect craftsmanship. And it is for his perfect, absolutely perfect, craftsmanship that Vermeer is praised and valued. He was one of those rare artists who carry a particular achievement as far as it can possibly be carried, to the stage beyond which it cannot possibly go and yet remain perfect. He knew the final secret of 'finish' in painting, and any artist later than Vermeer who has been much concerned with 'finish' – as many of the English Victorian painters were – appears mechanical and insipid. Nevertheless, when we grow enthusiastic over Vermeer's perfection as a craftsman, we must not forget that his success was due to his sensitive eye and his perfect taste, not simply to sleight of hand. Perfection of finish is only a virtue in a work of art which is in all respects worthy of it. Otherwise 'finish' is labour in vain; mere polish on a trumpery thing.

USING LIGHT

The National Gallery (London) owns two of Vermeer's rare paintings: one of a lady standing, the other of a lady seated, at the virginals, an instrument which preceded the modern piano. We can see from them how Vermeer used light; his love of blue (another of his favourite colours was a beautiful pale golden yellow); his interest in musical instruments and pictures – he obviously delighted in making paintings of paintings, either hanging on the walls or as decorations on articles of furniture, for he introduces them again and again; and his uncanny ability, alluded to before, to represent the texture of fabrics and substances. These National Gallery paintings are fairly elaborate, and it is easier to examine (even in the black and white print on Plate 10) one of Vermeer's simpler compositions in order to appreciate his mastery of 'tactile values', a term indicating those qualities in a picture which stimulate the imagination through our sense of touch, not solely through our eyes.

It is by stimulating our imagination in various ways that art serves us best. A good artist is not only exceptionally sensitive but is also able to communicate his sensitivity to others. If our sensibilities are dull, we remain under-developed and become no better than human clods. For a good many people that is a comfortable state. Even if they do not get much pleasure from life, at least they do not get much pain. A sensitive and imaginative person has all his faculties sharply alert: he sees more, hears more, tastes more, feels more; he thinks more, imagines more, understands more, enjoys more; fears more, hopes more, despairs more; admires more, despises more, loves more, hates more. It is not people that he hates and despises, but injustice, cruelty, meanness, ugliness. Those capable of experiencing all these sensations have a fuller, wider, deeper life, and in total a happier one. Those who do not desire such a life should keep away from paintings and other works of art, because that is the life to which art leads us by exercising all our faculties and sharpening all our sensibilities, through the stirring of imagination.

'THE COOK'

Vermeer's paintings delight our eyes, and they possess the finer virtue of communicating to us imaginatively, through a sharpened sense of touch, the 'feel' of everything shown in them. Let us consider *The Cook* (Rijksmuseum, Amsterdam) (see Plate 10). A buxom young Dutch woman of the peasant class stands beside a small covered table under a high window at our left of the picture. Behind her is a plain creamy-white wall with a row of decorated blue Delft tiles at floor-level. On the floor between her and the wall is a wooden warming box with a patterned top and one open side, holding a red earthenware crock. In front of the box is a wooden skewer. The cook wears an unbleached white linen head-dress of the sunbonnet type; a laced stuff bodice of dusty yellow with turned-up sleeves of another material lined with dull blue; a blue apron, folded up to the waist at one side, partially covers her skirt of dull red; and material of a similar blue hangs in irregular folds over the table edge. The cook is pouring milk from a red earthenware jug into a double-handled bowl of the same ware. Two loaves of coarse-textured bread lie in a flat open basket of interlaced wicker work on the table; pieces of broken bread lie beside it, loose on the dull greenish tablecloth. A blue jug with a handle and hinged lid has a bold raised pattern in self colour, the whole highly glazed. High up at the left, between the window and the back wall, hangs a closed, four-sided wicker basket with a domed lid; suspended near it on the other wall is a polished metal container.

Vermeer appears to have been fascinated equally by elegance (as in the National Gallery pictures) and by a bare simplicity (as in *The Cook* and several others). There is a definite pictorial reason for everything in *The Cook*, and nothing is superfluous.

ARRANGING THE OBJECTS IN A PICTURE

This is a convenient place to introduce a term often used by writers on paintings: *spatial relations*. 'Spatial' is, of course, the adjective derived from 'space', so the term at the end of the last sentence means *the relationship in space of the various objects appearing in a picture* – the placing of them in relation to one another and in relation to the whole surface-area of the picture. If an artist paints only one object in a picture he does not place it in the exact centre of the canvas, or panel, or wall-space (if he should happen to be painting direct on to a wall). We talk about 'dead centre' when we mean the very middle of a space, and it is a most expressive phrase if we apply it to painting. Anything placed alone in the exact centre of a picture does look 'dead', i.e. very dull and uninteresting.

AN EXPERIMENT TO TRY

If, however, the object is moved slightly to one side and slightly upward or downward – so long as the horizontal movement does not measure precisely the same as the vertical movement – it looks less dull and less uninteresting. This would be a test of the *spatial relation* of the single object to the whole picture-area. You can easily make such a test by cutting out an animal, or a house, or any simple thing from a newspaper or magazine picture, and then shifting it about on a sheet of plain paper until you find the spot which gives the most pleasing effect. If you then cut out several other objects which go well with whatever you chose first, you can place them all on the plain paper and move them about here and there until you find that you have spaced them pleasingly in relation to one another and in relation to the whole area of the paper. You will find that the size of the paper also needs to be either increased or lessened, according to the number and relative sizes of the cut-outs assembled on it. Furthermore, you will also find that if the cut-outs are placed at equal distances from one another and from the edges of the paper, the effect will be unpleasing to your eye and unsatisfying to your mind. If you group some of them at one side (but not, preferably, equidistant from each other) and put one or two at the other side, or just out of centre, the pattern will seem less 'dead'. In playing about thus with the cut-outs and the sheet of paper you will have been adjusting the *spatial relations* of the rough made-up picture. You will find, too, that there is almost no end to the variations you can get. If several people have been trying this experiment independently at the same time, and you compare the several results when each is satisfied with his own arrangement, you will discover that you like some much better than others.

THE IMPORTANCE OF SPACE

So it is with painters, even with good painters. One artist's pictures may be much more pleasing in this respect than another's, and we can get almost endless interest and fun from examining pictures with this matter of spatial relations in mind. Vermeer was brilliantly clever in his arrangement of figures and objects within the picture-area, and he was perhaps more daring than any other painter in deliberately leaving nearly blank spaces in his pictures; *nearly* blank, for by a wonderful instinct he always saved any space from a sense of emptiness. In *The Cook*, the box on the floor gives interest to what would otherwise have been a rather dull area of space, while the hanging objects fulfil a similar purpose in relation to the wall.

Simple though it is, this painting brings in six different sorts of fabric; three different kinds of earthenware; wood; brass; wicker; bread; milk. As our eyes dwell on each in turn, our sense of touch registers a different sensation. This may not happen to everyone who looks at Vermeer's paintings, since no two persons are alike in their registering apparatus. Some have a very acute sense of touch and their finger-tips are so very much alive that these become, as it were, ten extra eyes. If such people look at a Vermeer painting, *The Cook* for example, they not only see with their eyes the various fabrics and materials, they also feel at their finger-ends the differences of substance and texture and even the varying surface-temperatures. Without thinking about the matter in advance, they become aware as they look at the objects in this picture that the blue glazed jug would be cooler as well as smoother to the touch than the red earthenware vessels. And so also with the relative weights of the various objects. They 'feel', imaginatively, just how much muscular effort would be required to lift each.

However acute our sense of touch (or tactile sense) may be, we cannot get this delicate reaction from all paintings. Vermeer is exceptional in this respect, and his pictures have to be given very high marks for *tactile value*.

AN ARTFUL ARTIST

This is a wizardry peculiar to Vermeer among the Dutch 'Little Masters'. Pieter de Hooch has certain characteristics in common with Vermeer as a painter of domestic interiors, but he does not reach so high a general level. Our tactile sense is rarely stimulated by his paintings, and even if we try to meet de Hooch half-way by imagining how his fabrics and substances would feel we are not much helped by the painter. The National Gallery *Interior of a Dutch House* is fresh and cool and brilliant, but we do not get, as we do from Vermeer's pictures, the impression that we could walk all round the room and around the people in it. The serving maid in *Interior of a Dutch House* hardly looks like a three-dimensional figure standing in the space of the room, but, rather, like a coloured cut-out placed flat against the chimney-piece. Nor can we as easily persuade ourselves, as we can with Vermeer, that de Hooch's men and women are alive and breathing. They might have been enchanted and made motionless by some mischievous fairy. We note, too, that the curling scrap of paper lying on the black-and-white tiled floor in this painting has a sort of self-conscious smirk, as though it had been put there deliberately as 'a realistic touch' intended to impress the spectator. Vermeer's paintings are full of no less deliberate artifices – no artist could possibly be more artful. But artifice is not necessarily a fault in an artist; it is in fact the very means by which he creates his works. What marks out the greater artists from the lesser ones is that in the former the artifice is not noticed by us unless we make a detailed analysis of how the work was done. There is a saying that 'Art conceals art', but it would be nearer to the truth if we rewrote it as 'Art conceals artifice' – meaning that a perfect work of art is one which does not call our attention to how it was done.

De Hooch's most interesting and personal contribution to Dutch painting was his pictures of courtyards (backyards, we might call them) of small houses. Even in those the figures are static, but the placid atmosphere of one sort of domestic life in Holland is charmingly preserved in them.

Another side of the Dutch character is presented by Jan Steen, some of whose paintings remind us that seventeenth-century Holland was not composed wholly of elegant, placid, and simple people. There was tavern life as well as home life. There were noisy drunkards as well as peaceable, law-abiding, God-fearing citizens. Pictures of roistering scenes are common among both the Dutch and the Flemish painters, and among the latter it is at once a shock and a relief to turn from the detailed perfection of Jan van Eyck to the rough, full-blooded, and sometimes cruel scenes painted by Pieter Brueghel, and from Rubens's aristocratic style to his pictures of peasant festivals, with their lusty bank-holiday uproar. The Flemings usually impress us, rightly or not, as having been a more spiritually sensitive people than the Dutch, and it is therefore harder to reconcile these opposite sides of Flemish painting. But it requires all sorts of people to make a nation.

GOOD LIKENESSES

For beginners, portrait painting is perhaps the most difficult branch of art to understand and enjoy *as painting*. If we happen to know, either from personal acquaintance or from photographs, what the subject of a portrait is actually like in physical appearance, we are inclined to think more about whether it is a good likeness than whether it is a good painting. And if it is a portrait of someone who lived long ago but is not in the history books, we may think that because the subject is of no interest to us the painting must also be without interest. The National Portrait Gallery in London is not an exciting place when we are young, and even when we are older and know more about art we probably go a dozen times to the National Gallery next door to every once that we go to the portrait collection. There is a good reason for this. The National Portrait Gallery does not set out to be first of all a collection of great paintings, though it does contain many very fine ones. Its main purpose is to provide a pictorial record of famous British men and women, and it is therefore concerned to possess good likenesses rather than masterpieces of art. When a portrait is really great as a painting it more often goes to the National Gallery than to the Portrait Gallery, because its quality as a work of art is higher than its interest as a likeness. You might remark, at this point, that surely a portrait which is great as a painting must also be a good likeness. That brings us back to a matter touched upon earlier in this book (see pages 11–19): namely, that a great artist *sees into* his subject, and doesn't merely *see* it. We can agree that a good portrait painting should be a good likeness, so long as we also agree that what any person is *like* equals his physical appearance plus his mental ability plus his moral character. Very few of us would be bold enough to claim that, in this triple sense, we really know what our closest friends or even the members of our family are 'like'. A human being is like 'a book with seven seals' and it is only the penetrating vision of the greatest artists that can lay open its secrets. Yet we cannot always exclude a portrait from consideration as a work of art just because it does not convince us that it is a good character-study. Even if it lacks what some people call 'psychological penetration' – the ability to look into the mind and heart and to bring unseen qualities to the surface – it may still be lovely to look at.

A DASHING PORTRAIT

One of the most renowned portraits in the world is Frans Hals's *The Laughing Cavalier* (Wallace Collection, London). Its popularity is due in part to the soldier's handsome devil-may-care expression and in part to the exact copying in paint of the fine lace of his collar and cuffs. It is a triumph of bravado so far as the face is concerned, and the clothes 'look just like the real thing' (which is something the general public always likes in a picture). It is a dashing portrait of a dashing gentleman in a dashing manner by an artist who was in a dashing mood. For the taste of some, all this dash is rather too much of a good thing; they find its effect cloying and sickly, as though they had eaten too many chocolates at one time. Frans Hals was himself an uproarious creature who nevertheless had moods of sober quietness. He was also a very fine painter who painted best when he was not in a swaggering mood. By temperament he seems to have been what we might aptly call 'a human chameleon': he could adapt and change himself to become like the people he happened to be with at any moment. He swaggered with the swaggerers, boozed with the boozers, was sober with the sober. This made it possible for him to paint any type or class of person in the style exactly suitable for each. His colours and brushes seem to have had an almost miraculous ability to do whatever was appropriate to each different occasion. Even the paint seems to boast, or to hiccup, or to meditate and brood, according to the nature of the sitter. Hals therefore produced a varied succession of portraits in which the personality of each sitter is revealed almost as clearly as the face and clothes. Indeed, the clothes seem to be saturated with the wearer's personality. There are moments when Hals's portraits remind us of Rembrandt's, though the resemblance is neither close nor lasting. Rembrandt was a whole man – a unified person – as well as a giant of genius. Hals was like a swarming bagful of manikins, each one a dwarf of genius always within call to do the required job at the required moment. Rembrandt was always Rembrandt; Hals could be all things to all men. Taken together, however, these two men lifted seventeenth-century Dutch portrait-painting to a height unsurpassed at any time elsewhere.

OUT-OF-DOORS PAINTINGS

To portraits and interiors was added a third glory in this wonderful age of art in Holland: landscapes. At one time, Hobbema and Cuyp were greatly esteemed, but in the eyes of the present generation they are overshadowed by Jacob van Ruisdael, to whose pictures English landscape-painting is much indebted for the influence they had on John Constable in the early part of the nineteenth century.

We have seen in casual glimpses how Nature was at first admitted timidly into paintings by the Italian artists. From miniature vistas seen through small windows in the background of religious pictures, landscape scenes became larger and larger until sacred personages and incidents from the Bible and the lives of saints were placed in the foreground of sweeping stretches of countryside which filled all the remainder of the picture. At a later stage, the figures began to move *into* the landscape and to become interrelated with it. This was particularly so in paintings of pagan gods and goddesses and other mythological characters amid abundant foliage and beside running streams. But attention was for a long time still centred mainly on the figures. Landscape in itself was not regarded as an important branch of painting, though a few early artists (e.g. the Flemish Joachim Patinir, born in 1485) showed how little it need depend on the presence of human and animal figures. With Rubens (in Flanders) and Claude and Poussin (in France) in the seventeenth century, landscape became of major interest, yet it continued to be excused somewhat apologetically by the use of such titles as *Landscape: Marriage of Isaac and Rebecca; Landscape with Figures; Landscape with a Shepherd*, and so on; while in England as late as Gainsborough, well on in the eighteenth century, portraits and figure subjects were ranked high above landscape. It was not until Ruskin began, in *Modern Painters*, in 1843, to praise Turner's pictures for their 'truth to Nature' that English art-patrons ceased to look askance at landscape painters. Even Turner himself, as an intense admirer of Claude, followed in the early part of his career the 'landscape with figures' fashion.

Ruisdael and other Dutch landscapists of his time, however, reduced almost to vanishing point the space occupied by animate figures. In one typical Ruisdael painting, a man, a woman, and a child on a country road running through wheat-fields fill less than 1/400th part of the picture-space, and the farm buildings are almost hidden by a clump of trees at a bend of the road as it disappears in the middle distance. The land area, including the trees, takes up about a third of the picture, the remainder being given to one of those grand cloud-studies which are so distinctive in these quiet Dutch landscapes and, as a result of their influence on Constable, in his paintings also. Most of the finest English landscape paintings have been the work of men born in the eastern counties, in which the light and atmosphere are similar in quality to those of Holland. Turner is an exception, for he was born in London; but then Turner is an exception to almost every convenient rule.

6

Some Great Painters of Spain and France

THE National Gallery (London) catalogue includes works
by more than 120 Dutch painters. All but six of these did
their work in the seventeenth century and no doubt there
were scores, perhaps hundreds, more painting in Holland in
that amazing period, when pictures were so plentiful that
many of the painters found it hard to make a living unless
they took a bread-and-butter job of some kind. The few
mentioned in the last chapter are the most important, but
there were a large number of others whose paintings would
seem more impressive if there had been no Rembrandt and
Vermeer and Ruisdael to overshadow them.

In Spain things were altogether different. There, though
the outstanding period lasted about twice as long as in
Holland, the great artists were few (the National Gallery
catalogues no more than fifteen from the sixteenth century
to the nineteenth). Of those, three (El Greco, Velasquez,
and Goya) are in the front rank, and the names of four
others (Ribalta, Ribera, Zurbaran, and Murillo) are
familiar. Numbers may actually prove nothing, of course,
even when they appear to be proving much, and if we were
to probe down to a more commonplace but still respectable
level we should find it easy to make a much longer list of
Spanish painters. So far as the National Gallery is concerned, we have to remember that contact between Holland
and England was then much easier than between Spain and
England. Many pictures crossed from Holland to England,
where Dutch landscapes, especially, were liked in the eastern
counties and influenced two of the greatest English landscape painters, Gainsborough and Constable.

WE ARE ALL DIFFERENT

The Dutch are by nature a democratic and tranquil people. The Spanish are aristocratic and tormented. Both nations have suffered under foreign oppression and both have shaken themselves free. But while the Dutch freed themselves spiritually and mentally as well as politically, the Spanish failed to do so, and the signs suggest that they never will succeed. Historians trace the peculiarities of the Spanish character to the country's isolation from the rest of Europe by the barrier of the high Pyrenees on the northern land frontier and by sea elsewhere, though neither geography nor history, nor even religion, provides a wholly convincing explanation. The Catholic faith in Italy can be said to have softened the hearts of the people; in Spain it scorched their souls and made them fanatical. In Holland, foreign invasion bred determination; in Spain, vengefulness. Fanaticism and a desire for revenge may be bred by religion on the one hand and by oppression on the other, but only if the germ is already there. National as well as individual character develops from inborn qualities rather than from outside circumstances. Whether we like it or not, nations as well as persons differ a good deal from one another, and the differences would not be smoothed away by setting up one single government for the whole world. In art, such differences are a blessing. Nothing could be duller than a world in which painters everywhere painted in one single style. Fortunately that is unlikely ever to happen. There will always be differences of weather, if of nothing else, in the different regions of the earth, and painters must always be affected to some extent by the local weather because that affects the quality and intensity of light, upon which every painter depends.

Such matters open up large and important questions which we have no room to attempt to answer here. We must be content with noting that Spanish painting, for the most part, lacks that spirit of confident serenity found in much of

1. Prehistoric Painting in a Cave at Altamira, Spain: Mammoth Bison

2. Prehistoric Painting in a Cave at Valencia, Spain: Hunting Scene

3. Margaritone (late Byzantine): Madonna and Child (Detail). *National Gallery, London*

4. Artist Unknown: Elizabeth and the Child John. *Canterbury Cathedral*

5. Duccio: The Three Marys at the Tomb. *Siena*

6. Fra Angelico: The Annunciation. *Florence*

7. Botticelli: Head of Venus from 'Mars and Venus'.
National Gallery, London

8. Correggio: Head of Venus from
'Mercury Instructing Cupid Before Venus'.
National Gallery, London

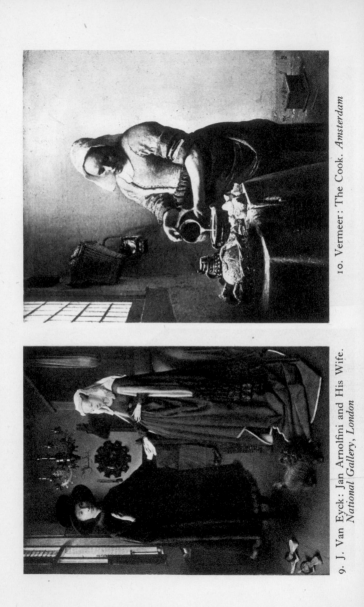

10. Vermeer: The Cook. *Amsterdam*

9. J. Van Eyck: Jan Arnolfini and His Wife.
National Gallery, London

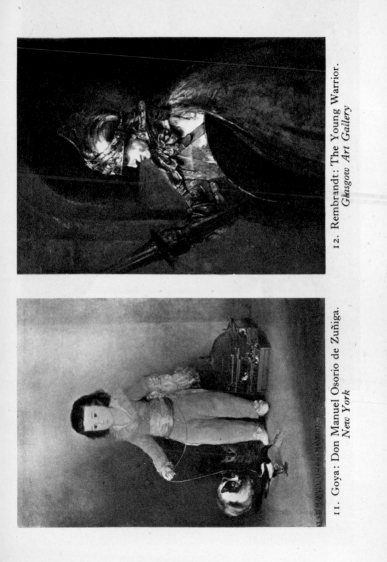

11. Goya: Don Manuel Osorio de Zuñiga.
New York

12. Rembrandt: The Young Warrior.
Glasgow Art Gallery

13. Velasquez: Pope Innocent X. *Rome*

14. Bellini: The Agony in the Garden. *National Gallery, London*

15. El Greco: The Agony in the Garden. *National Gallery, London*

16. Hogarth: The Graham Children. *Tate Gallery, London*

17. Reynolds: The Strawberry Girl. *Reproduced by permission of the Trustees of the Wallace Collection*

18. Gainsborough: The Painter's Daughters. *National Gallery, London*

19. Watteau: The Embarkation for Cythera. *Louvre, Paris*

20. Constable: Brighton Beach. *Victoria and Albert Museum, London*

21. ?Chardin: Still Life. *National Gallery, London*

22. Paul Cézanne: Still Life. *Oslo*

23. Turner: Interior at Petworth. *Tate Gallery, London*

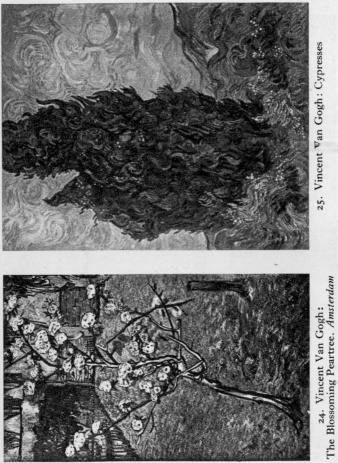

24. Vincent Van Gogh:
The Blossoming Peartree. *Amsterdam*

25. Vincent Van Gogh: Cypresses

26. Manet: Le Bar aux Folies-Bergère. *The Courtauld Institute, London*

27. Paul Nash: Encounter in the Afternoon. *Private Collection, London*

the art of other European countries. Religious painting at its highest level in Spain is either fanatical or so sternly spiritual as to seem inhuman; on its lower levels it is sentimental; while the best non-religious painting there is often either haughtily aristocratic or bitterly satirical. These adjectives are, however, explanatory, not words of condemnation, for El Greco, Velasquez, and Goya, besides being the greatest Spanish painters, are among the whole world's best.

NOT A SIMPLE SUM

El Greco was a Greek born in the island of Crete, where he became steeped in the Byzantine spirit (see pages 40–50) before he visited and worked for a while in Italy, absorbing from the Venetian painters their love of colour. He reached Spain round about 1575 and passed most of the remainder of his life in Toledo, where he died some forty years afterwards, having painted both for the Church and for the Court, not always to the liking of either. In formality, severity, and spiritual intensity, his paintings are Byzantine; in their richness of colour, Venetian; in their aristocratic aloofness, Spanish; but their essential genius can be traced to no one but El Greco himself. They do not represent a sum in simple addition: Byzantium+Venice+Spain; they are very much more than a bit of this and a bit of that and a dash of the other.

El Greco's paintings are sometimes said to belong to the *baroque* style, which means (see page 71) that type of art dominated by the fascination of movement. Artists who painted in the baroque style often regarded movement as an end in itself, and set out to prove that inanimate stuff, whether paint or stone or metal or wood or ivory, could be so represented as to give the illusion of 'livingness'. Baroque art was much favoured by the Jesuits, for whom it had a spiritual significance, suggesting in the towering groups of figures found in their sculpture and carved ivories the upward aspiration of human beings in their progress from earth to heaven. In so far as El Greco's paintings have a remarkable quality of organic movement – seeming to have a life of their own, as the human body has through the working of its various organs – they, too, may be called baroque. Yet they differ importantly, since they have a subtle rhythm instead of the crude undulation and monotonous serpentining which is the distinguishing feature of much baroque art. El Greco's greatness was largely due to his mastery of rhythm.

RHYTHM

Now while we all *know* what rhythm is, because our lives from birth to death are controlled by it, it is very difficult to *say* what rhythm is, just as it is difficult to say what life is. However, an attempt must be made here to put it into words, because the full enjoyment of art in any form – paintings, sculpture, music, poetry, or whatever – depends so much upon an understanding of the nature of rhythm that it is not enough to be vaguely conscious of rhythm as 'a something'.

The simplest definition of rhythm would be 'flowing movement', but that is too simple. Not every flowing movement is rhythmical in the true sense. If we make a switchback in which each upward curve reaches exactly the same height and each downward curve the same depth, a car running along it will have a flowing motion, but not a rhythmical one. The regular up-and-down movement quickly becomes boring to anyone riding in the car as well as to anyone watching it. To save it from being monotonous it would be necessary to vary the levels and gradients of the risings and dippings. That would also vary the distances from peak to peak, with consequent variation in the time it would take the car to run from one peak to the next. The switchback would then be more exciting to the rider and more interesting to the watcher. But the switchback example is not really a good one, because there would be a certain amount of jerking each time the car started to go up an incline; and jerking or any sudden arresting of movement destroys rhythm. Rhythm must be *unbroken movement*, whatever degree of variety may enter into it. The switchback does, however, help us to grasp two important factors in regard to rhythm: (i) that the flowing movement must have *variation in space;* (ii) that it must have *variation in time.* It must not be obviously regular.

RIPPLES ON A STREAM

A simple example of rhythm in space can be created by dropping a stone into a quiet stream on a windless day. When we look down on the water we see a number of enlarging concentric circles rippling away from the spot where the stone fell in; if it were possible to cut a section through the rippling circles on the water and watch them at eye level, we should find not only variation in the distances between the crests of the ripples as they move away from the centre but also variation in their height. All this could easily be shown in a diagram, and it would give an elementary example of rhythm visible to the eye (*visual rhythm*). If our ears were sensitive enough, we could also detect variation in the time elapsing between the formation of one ripple and the next. That would be rhythm distinguishable by the ear (*audible rhythm*). Visual rhythm is present in good paintings and good sculpture; audible rhythm in good music.

So far we have dealt only with simple rhythm – too simple to be of service in art.

Let us now recall the times when we have sat by the sea as the tide was coming in. One of Shakespeare's sonnets begins:

> Like as the waves make towards the pebbled shore,
> So do our minutes hasten to their end. . . .

The rhythm of the sea is not unlike the rhythm of life. Our

emotions of love and anger flood in like the tide and ebb more gently, as the tide does. Life itself is an incoming tide while we are young; it rises to high-tide mark when we reach maturity; it ebbs as we grow old. The rhythm of life, however, is infinitely more varied than that of the sea. Some of us develop faster than others, reach maturity at a different age, grow old at a different pace. That is the varying rhythm of the years. There is also the rhythm of experience. Some people lead 'fuller lives' (as we say) than others: they have more friends and wider interests; perhaps they travel more; some have children, others do not. The rhythm of life is affected by all these differing circumstances.

TIDES AND SEASONS

The tides of the ocean have a less complex rhythm; yet, even so, if we happen to live near the coast throughout the year we know that the seasons and the weather affect the tides, which are higher and stronger at one part of the year than at others; storms fling waves mountains high, the wind whips the wave-crests; at other times, on calm, sunny, cloudless days, we say 'the sea is like glass', though of course it never is – it is always in movement, flowing in, flowing out, moved by fixed and/or drifting currents. High-tide times alter day by day. The time can be calculated long in advance, but though we are able to say 'High tide will be at 11.15 this morning', we cannot put a stick on a certain spot representing yesterday's high-tide mark and say with certainty 'At 11.15 this morning the tide will reach this point exactly, neither an inch more nor an inch less.' Nevertheless, there is some governing influence which enables us to be certain that the tide will come in each day and will go out each day. So, also, we know that the seasons will return each year, though the first real day of spring in England is hardly ever the twenty-first of March, as the calendar would have us believe. And how very much less interesting the year would be if we always knew that on such and such a day we should have such and such weather. There is a governing rhythm of the tides and seasons, but no exact uniformity, no monotonously regular pattern. We may well heave a sigh and say 'Thank goodness!' Variety is as necessary as breath.

In rhythm, then, there is (*a*) flowing movement; (*b*) variation of movement; (*c*) some governing influence which keeps the whole thing under control and prevents it all from leaving the rails or running down. Rhythm is everywhere in human life from beginning to end, as well as in the seasons of the year and the tides of the ocean. The 'governing influence' is usually called God, but many prefer to call it Nature, or the Life Force, or by some other name.

A LOOK AT BALLET

Let us come back to art; but not, for the moment, straight back to paintings.

Most people now agree that ballet should be included among the fine arts, and it happens to be a form of art that large audiences enjoy very much indeed at the present time. It happens also to be a form of art in which rhythm is probably the most important factor of all: rhythm of sound, i.e. *audible rhythm*, in the music; rhythm of movement, i.e. *visual rhythm*, in the dancing and miming. It is with visual rhythm only that we are concerned in painting, so we will pass by the music of ballet, and concentrate attention on the movements of the dancers. Ballet enthusiasts often use the word 'line' when they are praising dancers: they say, for example, 'Her "line" is marvellous!' They mean that the dancer's rhythm of movement is beautiful. When we are watching a *prima ballerina*, although her movements might be said to begin at her toes and end at her finger-tips, the pleasure we get comes very largely from the fact that she makes us imagine that her movements do not begin at all and do not end at all. Movement appears to flow into her

feet and to flow from her hands after it has passed rhythmi-
cally through her whole body – as though the rhythm of
movement were some part of a universal rhythm which is
everywhere, always; without beginning and without end.
That is the mystery and miracle of rhythm – that it seems to
be an aspect of eternal beauty; not something confined to this
world of space and time, but something which flows endlessly
through the universe, we know not whither nor whence
nor why.

PATTERN AND DESIGN

One other point about ballet before we pass on. The
movements of dancers are made in the three dimensions of
space (as well as in the dimension of time – they 'keep time'
to the music). Their movements in space are (i) from side to
side of the stage; (ii) from back to front of the stage; (iii)
vertical – in leaping and elevation. If we think of the pros-
cenium arch of the stage as a picture frame, the rhythm of
the dancers arises from a complicated pattern of movements
across, *up*, and *into the depth of* the stage picture. If they
moved in one direction (or dimension) only, like figures on a
frieze, their dancing, however finely rhythmical in that single
dimension, would be less interesting than it is when they
move freely in three dimensions. A frieze effect was given
intentionally in the ballet danced to Debussy's *L'Après-Midi
d'un Faune*, and very attractive it was, but we should quickly
tire and lose interest if other ballets were treated in the same
manner. We shall be helped further to appreciate rhythm in
paintings if we keep in mind that dancers in ballet are not
confined to movements in unison: they are not all making
the same movement at the same time always. When they are
– as in certain *corps de ballet* passages in *Les Sylphides*, for
example – they may be creating a lovely rhythmical *pattern*,
but even that would become monotonous if it went on for
long. In the more complex passages in ballet there is dancing in harmony, the carrying out simultaneously of differing

movements by the various people on the stage, all interweaving to produce a rhythmical *design*.

'Pattern' and 'design' are commonly used as interchangeable words, but it will help to avoid confusion if we reserve 'pattern' for an arrangement of lines (or of movements) in two dimensions only, and 'design' for any arrangement of lines or movements in the three dimensions – by which, when speaking of a painting, we mean height, width, and depth. The canvas or whatever other material is used to paint on has, of course, only height and width, so the third dimension (when the artist requires it, which the Byzantines and certain oriental painters did not) has to be created by the means referred to on page 50.

RHYTHM THAT QUICKENS OUR IMAGINATION

In paintings there can be simple *rhythm of line*, as in Fra Angelico's *The Annunciation* (see pp. 57–8), where the artist's arrangement of curved lines creates in us as spectators the impression of flowing movement mainly in the dimension of width, though to a lesser degree in the dimension of height also. As we look at the angel's wing in the foreground we do not feel that the rhythm of line ends above the angel's right shoulder, nor, at the other end, at the point where the wing-tip passes behind the column. The artist quickens our imagination to receive the sensation that the edge of the wing is a visible section of a rhythmic curve which flows on invisibly at both ends. In this painting there is scarcely any representation of rhythm in depth. The artist meant to concentrate attention on the figures of Mary and the angel; he did not want the spectator's eyes to be led away into the background.

Such simple rhythm of line was even more marked in Byzantine paintings, where the emphasis was strongly on a flat two-dimensional pattern, to the neglect of solid three-dimensional design.

From simple rhythm of line we go on to *compound rhythm of mass*, which is what we find in the work of great painters. Rhythm of mass is most evident when the artist has a strong feeling for the bulk and weight of solid objects, as Michelangelo had for well-proportioned human bodies.

FIRE IN HIS SOUL

In El Greco's paintings the emphasis is sometimes on simple rhythm of line, sometimes on compound rhythm of mass; sometimes there is changing emphasis as between parts of the same picture. This made it possible for him to produce visually through a painting an effect like that produced audibly by a great composer in a symphony. There was certainly a fire alight in his soul and imagination, and this gives a special energy to the rhythm in his paintings. There is rhythmic force as well as rhythmic flow. They are not like a quiet stream but like an irresistible ocean tide.

If you look at El Greco's painting called *The Agony in the Garden* (National Gallery, London) – Plate 15 – you will find your eyes moving around the curved masses of rock, around the masses of cloud, around the outlines of the hills and trees in the background at the right, and around the curving folds of the robes of the figures: around ... around ... around; not round and round in circles, however, but with an in-and-out twining movement. Many of El Greco's paintings have the same effect of causing our eyes to follow his curving masses and swirling lines. The consequence is that the whole picture seems to be in a state of continuous rhythmical movement in all three dimensions, ebbing and flowing and pulsating like the blood in our veins. The greatness of El Greco's paintings does not lie so much in what they give us to look at, as in what they compel us to feel; and their power over our feelings comes from the painter's mastery of rhythm.

Several great painters have taken the Agony in the Garden as a subject, and when we look at pictures of this bitter episode in the life of Christ we are usually more visually conscious of the garden than spiritually conscious of the agony, though it is the purpose of the New Testament narrative to bring home to us the awfulness of what Christ was enduring at that time. El Greco is the one artist who has really conveyed that purpose in a picture. He painted the agony rather than the garden; the tragedy rather than merely the place where the tragedy happened. When we compare his painting with Bellini's (see Plate 14) dealing with the same episode, we see at once that whereas the latter is more realistic visually, El Greco puts spiritual intensity first and does not attempt to represent the garden realistically. The strange-looking cave in which the sleeping disciples are confined is like no cave we have seen, except in Byzantine paintings which El Greco must have remembered.

PROPHET AND PAINTER

In El Greco's pictures there is rhythm of mood, rhythm of colour, rhythm of mass, rhythm of line; but his greatness as an imaginative artist and master craftsman must not blind us to what was, after all, the real driving-force of his genius: namely, his spiritual passion and Catholic fervour. There is an almost fanatical power in his works, as though he were more a prophet than a painter. He would not have wished to be praised for the strange and troubling beauty of his pictures, but to be judged by their effect on men's souls. He was a preacher using paint instead of words as the raw material of his sermons, and we could well believe that his message was 'Flee from the wrath to come!' We sense that mood even in his famous landscape, *Toledo in a Storm*, where the livid green earth and the somehow ghostly buildings create the ominous impression that they will be overwhelmed and destroyed by fire and brimstone which seems about to pour from the terrible threatening clouds that boil above the city.

A PAINTER OF MAGNIFICENCE

Born about half a century later than El Greco, Velasquez, though a native of Seville, came of a wealthy Portuguese family. For the most part of his working life he painted at the Spanish Court for Philip IV. Velasquez seems to have been an exceptionally attractive man, and he was certainly a magnificent painter, with an aristocratic temper which shows in his pictures. He no more belonged to the common run of mankind than El Greco did, but worldly ceremonial and display engrossed him, not religion and its ritual. Each of these two painters executed at least one portrait of a high Church dignitary, and it so happened that Velasquez was much influenced in his painting of Pope Innocent X by El Greco's of the Grand Inquisitor. The principal colours in both pictures are scarlet and white, though it is interesting to note that whereas El Greco used a dead white, Velasquez preferred a rich creamy white which has the immediate effect of giving his portrait a feeling of warmth. In every respect Velasquez's picture is warmingly human, while El Greco's is deliberately chilling, as befits the portrait of a man who had sent unnumbered heretics to an agonizing death. Both portraits are great paintings; both have a typically Spanish air of aristocratic remoteness and isolation – the austere aristocracy of the spirit in the one instance, the haughty aristocracy of social privilege in the other. We cannot easily believe that either painter was deeply interested in the personality of the man he was portraying. As we look at El Greco's Inquisitor we think not of a human being but of a vessel of wrath. As we look at the Pope's portrait we think how much Velasquez must have enjoyed painting such a magnificent object. (See Plate 13.)

It is usual to speak of a painter's *subjects*, but to Velasquez all subjects were *objects*. When he painted the young daughter of the king three times he was chiefly interested in the different dresses she wore. The dresses were objects to paint; she was little more than a *mannequin* displaying the dresses, and displaying them magnificently. So we have the *Infanta Margarita Teresa in Red*, the *Infanta Margarita Teresa in Green*, the *Infanta Margarita Teresa in Blue*. They are wonderful paintings of a little girl in fancy dresses, but we do not think of them as wonderful portraits of a child. Oddly enough, we are unlikely to rate this indifference to human character as a fault in Velasquez, even if it suggests to us some sluggishness of imagination in him. We are so dazzled by his brilliance – which is a solid brilliance, not a shallow flashy one – as to feel compensated for whatever other qualities he lacked. For all his aloof and aristocratic temper – or shall we say because of it? for a true aristocrat is one who resists contamination by what is base – Velasquez as a painter was an honest workman thoroughly absorbed in his job. If he had been a carpenter that last phrase would be an acceptable and honourable epitaph for him. It is no less honourable, though perhaps rarer, for a Court painter and a genius.

AN ARTIST OF PASSION AND PITY

Velasquez died in 1660, Goya was born in 1746. He was, in his own entirely different way, as much a seer and a visionary as El Greco was. He came from the bottom layer of society; yet, considered as a painter and according to the qualities of his work, he was no less an aristocrat than Velasquez, and like Velasquez he became Court painter. If his brilliance was less honestly solid than that of Velasquez, Goya had more insight and more feeling for human beings. His pictures of children – though he, too, loved fine clothes – are portraits first and clothes-paintings afterwards. In his painting of the little boy (*Don Manuel Osorio de Zuñiga*) in a vivid scarlet suit with a white silk and lace sash, the colour leaps at us the moment we set eyes on the picture, yet we find ourselves the next moment thinking not about the suit or the cleverness of Goya's painting of it but the enchanting face of the child; and then about the three cats, and the magpie, and the cage full of birds, all of which are on the floor around the little boy's feet. (See Plate 11.)

The centre of interest for Goya was always the liveness of living creatures. He lived through times when Spain was tortured by war, as she often has been, and among his most widely known works is a series of drawings called *The Disasters of War*. Terrible though they are, there runs through all of them a deep feeling of pain and pity for those who suffer, as well as of passionate indignation and hatred towards the makers of war. Goya was a man of torrential human passions as El Greco was of spiritual passions. He could not stand away from his subjects and look at them from the outside, as Velasquez could, keeping his private feelings separate from his public paintings. Goya's own personality gets into all of them, and since he could be by turns tender, coarse, gentle, brutal, cynical, compassionate, sensual, refined, his range is wider than that of the other two who share with him the peak of Spanish painting.

HOW PAINTING BEGAN IN FRANCE

Painting in France began in the same way as in Flanders – with richly coloured miniatures for the decoration of religious books, often for wealthy noblemen. There were also artists working on larger paintings, such as altar-pieces for churches, but for several centuries French art was more firmly attached than that of any other country to the service of kings and aristocrats. Several of the greatest French painters had little connexion with their own country after early years; and although in art catalogues and other books they are described as belonging to the 'French School', such men as Poussin and Claude spent so much time in Italy and developed so strong a liking for Italian paintings that there is little in their pictures to mark them out as Frenchmen. In fact, until the eighteenth century, most pictures painted by French artists were very little different in style from foreign ones. This has caused some confusion even among the experts, who still dispute whether *The Wilton Diptych* (one of the most attractive early pictures in the National Gallery, London) is French or English.

The French are usually considered to be a logical rather than an imaginative people; they trust more to common sense than to romantic ideas. We say that their literature and art are more 'classical' than 'romantic', and as those two words are often used in relation to works of art it will be worth while taking a little time here to discover something of what the words imply.

When people speak of the 'Classical Age' they refer principally to the period when ancient Greece produced great works of sculpture and architecture, usually in combination, of which the magnificent temple known as the Parthenon, at Athens, was the chief. Whether they were putting up buildings or carving statues or arranging their own lives, the ancient Greeks thought first of *proportion* and *balance*, which we can sum up in the one word 'form'. Their philosophers believed that a 'good' man was one in whom there was no excess of either virtues or faults. They would not have agreed with Christian people who believe that the only good life is an absolutely faultless one. The Greeks would have said that to try to be faultless is to try to be better than human nature permits; and, therefore, that a person who seeks to be faultless is in danger of becoming guilty of spiritual pride – a sin that (in their opinion) the gods punish severely. The proud man climbs to a height and then is brought crashing down. The ancient Greeks would not have been in any way surprised by the downfall of Hitler, nor by the lean years that have befallen Britain.

They would have regarded Hitler as such a monster of pride and ambition that the gods were certain to punish him – or, rather, to cause him to punish himself by losing control of his own desires, which toppled over and destroyed him. Britain, they would have said, was bound to suffer sooner or later because of extravagant pride in her commercial prosperity in the nineteenth century. The Greeks would not have agreed that there is any real difference between political pride, financial pride, and spiritual pride. To them, pride of any kind was always as fragile as a toy balloon, which is certain to burst when it is puffed up beyond a certain point.

Just as in spiritual and practical life the ancient Greeks believed that men must keep themselves within bounds and strike a balance between 'mighty opposites', so also they believed in preserving a balance in art. They were opposed to any kind of extravagance in any department of human activity. Their art was controlled and balanced and orderly.

NOT TOO MUCH OF ANYTHING

Unfortunately a somewhat false impression of Greek art has come down to us. In their architecture and sculpture (very few ancient Greek paintings have survived) a great deal of white stone and marble was used. This has led us to think of classical art as cold and rigid, but it was much less so than is commonly supposed. The Greeks put plenty of colour on to their buildings and statuary, and gold and precious or semi-precious stones were used to decorate the latter. In course of time the weather wore away the colour, and the gold and other valuables were stolen. Nevertheless, although the popular view of ancient classical art may be out of focus, the word 'classical' has been adopted as a convenient label for the kind of art in which form and line and well-con-. trolled feeling are the chief characteristics. In contrast stands 'romantic' art, in which (when painting is considered) outlines are softer, colours are richer and tend to melt into one another, and the picture stirs our emotions more than it stimulates our minds. The two heads of Venus, one by Botticelli, the other by Correggio (Plates 7 and 8), give some impression of the difference between the two kinds of painting, though Botticelli was by no means entirely classical in spirit. We can see, however, that his head of Venus is controlled within firm lines, whereas the other has no such control. If it were possible to record on a diagram exactly what happens when we look at one of these pictures and then at the other, we should almost certainly find that Botticelli's appeals more to the mind and Correggio's more to the emotions. For the time being it will be enough to remember, as a rough and ready definition, that *classical art relies mainly on form,* and *romantic art mainly on feeling.*

There is no need to take sides with one of the opposing parties who think either that classical art is superior to romantic art, or romantic art is superior to classical art. Both can be good. Classical art is bad only when it is so cold and rigid as to become lifeless; and then, of course, it is classical only in name, because (as we have noted above) the essence of classicism is *balance* – neither too little nor too much of anything. Romantic art is bad only when emotion is allowed to get so out of control that it slops over into sentimentality.

When art in France is truly French it is formal (classical) rather than emotional (romantic). In this connexion we should remember that inasmuch as the ancient Romans took over their art very largely at second hand from the Greeks, a strong classical tradition lasted for centuries in Rome and spread not only to other places in Italy, but also to more distant parts of Europe, including France, where Roman civilization rooted itself in the path of Caesar's triumphant legions. Romanticism has at intervals broken into French art, but there has been again and again a return to classicism, as though that were the natural French mode.

The earliest master in the history of French painting (excluding the medieval miniaturists) was Jean Fouquet (fifteenth century), who produced works in which form and a cool logical style are the chief factors. Fouquet himself began as a miniaturist illuminating manuscripts, but after a stay in Rome he returned to his own country to become Court painter to Charles VII. We have already found that painters elsewhere had taken to making the Madonna's face resemble that of some ordinary young woman of their own time and district – in Italian pictures there is often a likeness to Italian peasant girls – so it is not surprising that when Fouquet came to paint a *Virgin and Child* he should have taken as his model a woman who had helped him to get his post at Court. This woman was the king's favourite, Agnes Sorel. She was beautiful, but she had a bad influence on Charles VII and was hated by the French people, so it shocked them to find her posing as the Queen of Heaven in Fouquet's painting.

COOL AND CALCULATING

A 'classical' artist, however, does not let his feelings run away with him in his art. He is cool and calculating *as an artist*, whatever he may be in himself as a man. We may not know what Fouquet thought about Agnes Sorel's character, but we can imagine that when he set out to paint this *Virgin and Child* he wanted to make the Virgin appear as beautiful as possible, and Agnes Sorel was probably the most beautiful woman he knew. What could be more natural, then, than that he should paint her portrait in this picture? No doubt he also thought it sensible to please her, and he knew it would please his employer, the king. These are not high motives for a painter of religious subjects, but again we should remind ourselves that a 'classical' artist is interested mainly in the formal side of his art. He does not use art to express either his own private feelings or to stir ours; nor is art to him a means of sermonizing or of teaching moral lessons. His only object if he is a painter is to paint well, not to paint pictures that will inspire spectators to earn good-conduct marks. The only thing that mattered to Fouquet the painter was that Agnes Sorel was beautiful to look at. She is exceedingly beautiful in his painting, and the whole painting is beautiful. Yet the beauty in it is cold, even though there are six angels in vivid red (besides two in deep blue) round about the chair in which the woman is seated with the child on her lap. Her skin colour is so pale that she appears more like a statue than a flesh-and-blood human being. Everything in the picture is firmly and sharply out-lined; each colour is kept severely separate from its neigh-bouring colour; there is no soft blending of tones such as we find in 'romantic' paintings (see, again, Correggio's head of Venus).

A MASTER OF DRAWING

This preference for clean firm lines comes out elsewhere in French painting, notably in the works of Jacques Louis David (he must not be confused with the Flemish Gerhardt David) who became Dictator of Art at the time of the Revolution and under Napoleon later; and also in those of David's pupil, Ingres, who was one of the greatest draughts-men ever known. Some painters are good colourists but bad draughtsmen. By that we mean that they paint the surfaces of things very pleasingly so far as colour arrangement and colour relations are concerned, but that they are not success-ful in representing the shape or the internal structure of figures and objects. We then say that such-and-such a painter 'can't draw'. When he paints a portrait he does not seem to know enough about human anatomy – about where the bones and muscles are beneath the skin, or about the way in which the human skeleton is jointed – and the picture therefore looks flabby and unsupported, even though it may have surface beauty. This was an occasional weakness with Reynolds, who was in other respects one of the greatest

English portrait-painters. Ingres was a fine colourist, and exceptionally skilled in suggesting the texture of silks and shawls and various kinds of materials, as well as of the human skin-surface, but first and foremost he was a master draughtsman. It is useful and pleasant to look occasionally at uncoloured photographs of his paintings, in order to be able to enjoy the firm shapes and excellent designs without having our attention drawn away to the colours and textures. Yet in spite of his remarkable talents Ingres is not in the front rank of great painters. He falls midway between two styles: he is half classical, half not. The non-classical half is not 'romantic' either. On one side of his nature he was somewhat like an overfed cat in an overheated room – beautiful, but softened by a crude taste for luxury. On the other side he was as strictly devoted to painting as an earnest monk is to prayer.

A GOLDEN DREAM-WORLD

These contradictory qualities in Ingres in the nineteenth century resemble the contradictory nature of much French painting, particularly that of the eighteenth century, when Watteau produced those lovely pictures for which the general descriptive title *fêtes-galantes* is used. In the artificial French society of that period, before its exquisite but wasteful world was swept away by the Revolution, life had seemed like a perpetual open-air fancy-dress party for feasting and flirtation amid leafy groves and flowery gardens, where the air was filled with the music of lutes and running streams and youthful laughter. It was a golden dream-world which ended in a nightmare that was all too real. But while the dream lasted it was painted in all its charming make-believe by Watteau, Fragonard, Pater, Boucher, and others.

The most famous painting of that kind is Watteau's *Embarkation for Cythera* (The Louvre, Paris – see Plate 19), in

which light-hearted gallants and their ladies are seen starting off in a dream-boat for the island of love, which looms
in the distance through a golden haze. Though the picture
is like a rapturous song to Romance, it is not a true example
of 'romantic' painting. It is romantic in appearance, but not
in feeling. We get from it the impression that Watteau held
aloof from the kind of life of indulgence he was depicting,
regarding it critically as mere make-believe – lovely but
heartless, and therefore incapable of stirring his own emotions, or ours. Because Watteau recorded this artificial phase
of contemporary French society without being taken in by
it, his paintings have a serious quality which is missing from
those of Boucher and others of the time. Those artists convince us that they were flattering and pandering to the
ruinous frivolity reflected in their pictures. Their work lacks
both the underlying sincerity of Watteau's and the insight
into character which is shown in his paintings of single
figures and in his many admirable small drawings. (There
are fine examples of the latter in the British Museum Print
Room.)

At this point we can leave French Painting for a while.
There will be more to say about it later, in the chapters on
Modern Paintings.

7

English Paintings

IT has so often been said that the English (though not the
Scots, the Welsh, or the Irish) are an inartistic and unimaginative people, that the English have themselves come
to believe the accusation. They are told that they have no
vision, that they are more concerned about their pockets
than about their minds and souls. Since they are a modest
and a docile people,[1] full of self-distrust and slow to give
offence, it seldom occurs to them to point out that the
English have had not only the greatest poet of all time but
also more great poets than all other countries put together:
Chaucer, Spenser, Marlowe, Shakespeare, Milton, Pope,
Blake, Wordsworth, Shelley, Keats, Byron, Tennyson,
Browning, as well as many secondary poets who would be
ranked among the greatest in any other country.

The Italians have been supreme in painting, the Germans
in music, the English in poetry; and poetry requires at least
as high a quality of imagination and thought as any other
art. The truth of the matter is that the collective imagination
of a nation tends to flow most readily along a single main
channel. That of the English has run in the channel of
poetry.

This does not mean that nothing important, or even nothing great, appears outside the main channel of a nation's
genius. Italy, in addition to being supreme in the number of
first-rate painters she has produced, also had in Dante one
of the supreme poets of all time; and she has had excellent
musicians. So, also, Germany had Goethe as a great poet,
and Dürer and Holbein as great painters, in addition to the
geniuses among her composers of music.

1. Until someone tries to bully or oppress them. Then they become as
stubborn as mules, as tenacious as bulldogs, as cunning as serpents, and
as courageous as lions.

In England there have been a few painters of such outstanding importance that they would be in any list of the world's great artists. Hogarth is in a class by himself, for no other painter anywhere has produced quite the kind of pictures in which he excelled. Reynolds and Gainsborough would be in the list of the world's great portrait-painters. Gainsborough, Constable, and Turner are among the finest landscape-painters. For pure fiery imagination in landscape painting no one has equalled Turner. Blake stands alone as a visionary painter. When these six painters are added to the many great poets among their countrymen, with Wren as a very great architect, and Byrd and Purcell as fine composers, it is plain that the English have little cause to feel inferior in artistic achievement when they are compared with any other nation whatsoever.

PAINTING BEGAN LATE IN ENGLAND

For a long time it was usual to say that English painting began with Hogarth in the eighteenth century, centuries later than elsewhere in Europe. This is only true in so far as Hogarth may be said to have introduced an original style which is more typically English than that of any other painter born or working in England, where artists had been active since the Middle Ages as decorators of churches and other buildings, as illuminators of manuscripts, and as portrait-painters. But the country went through long periods of disturbance which were not favourable to the production and preservation of paintings. Pestilences such as the Black Death, internal strife due to revolt and the Plantagenet wars, religious upheavals, threats of foreign invasion, the trouble with kings which led to the struggle between the Royalists and the Cromwellians and later to the importation of William of Orange to displace James II – all this meant that until the end of the seventeenth century there was little feeling of settlement or sense of security. It is of course a fact that many masterpieces were painted in Italy during troubled times, but the Italian temperament is more buoyant than that of the English. Moreover, strife in Italy was often a local affair, and artists moved freely from one centre to another, while art in Italy was also much more of a business, a normal way of earning a living, than it could be in England. Italian artists had the patronage of the popes and cardinals and lesser dignitaries of the Church, and of princes and dukes, and other wealthy men. The demand for works of art – pictures, statues, churches and palaces, fountains, gold and silver ware, jewellery – was so widespread and continuous that with few exceptions artists did not spend their lives in the solitude of private studios, but amid the bustling busyness of workshops, or out on a job in a church or elsewhere with apprentices and assistants helping them.

In Italy and on the Continent generally, art was accepted as a necessity, required for the beautification of life. In England, however, many people have never escaped from the belief that art is a luxury, and that artists are peculiar – and not very nice! We usually think of the Puritans as a sect which sprang up in the seventeenth century, but there has always been a strong vein of puritanism – of cold suspicion of colour and gaiety and beauty – running through English history. Abroad, art is welcomed with open arms; in England it has to battle for a place in national life, and to maintain a running fight against those who do not hesitate to pull down beautiful buildings or to sell national art-treasures for export.

At this point we may seem to be agreeing with those who say that the English have neither soul nor imagination; but a nation must not be judged, though it often is, from the least favourable angle. It is just to admit that art in England has been hampered by puritan austerity, and by commercial indifference; yet it is also just to claim that, in spite of such handicaps, England has been rich in artistic genius.

English Paintings

If, then, painting in England counted for comparatively little until the eighteenth century the reasons may be found in the history books rather than in anything directly to do with art. Many church paintings were destroyed at the Reformation and during the Civil War; many others were hidden under whitewash in Puritan times and have only recently been uncovered. These early English paintings in churches and colleges are of great interest (even though they may not be very important as works of art) because, while they link up with the stiffness of the Byzantine school in general style, in feeling they have an informal and almost homely quality which makes us regard the figures in them as human beings rather than as spiritual personages. Whether the painters were Englishmen or aliens we cannot know for certain, but it is pleasant to imagine that when we look at the *Head of Christ* in the Winchester Cathedral painting, at the *Head of St Faith* (Westminster Abbey), and at the *Elizabeth and the Child John* (Canterbury Cathedral crypt) we are getting an impression of what people living in England in the twelfth and thirteenth centuries were like. However stiff and formal may be the pose of the mother and child in the last-named painting (see Plate 4), we do not have to go far in an English street to-day before seeing, perhaps in a bus queue, some woman whose slightly strained and anxious face reminds us of that of the Canterbury Elizabeth.

HOMELY PICTURES

The homely, human feeling which, rightly or wrongly, may be read into these church wall-paintings, has been a frequently recurring note in English painting since the Middle Ages. It can indeed be singled out as the distinguishing quality in English pictorial art. The native English genius keeps close to everyday matter-of-fact things; it either represents the ordinary commonplace atmosphere and experiences of normal life, or accepts the commonplace as a starting-point and transforms it into something new and strange.

> Earth's crammed with heaven
> And every common bush afire with God.

. . . . . .

> . . . the meanest flower that blows can give
> Thoughts that do often lie too deep for tears.

So wrote Elizabeth Barrett Browning and Wordsworth. Even Blake, our most visionary painter and poet, saw his angels on Peckham Rye. To him, anything, however lowly, could be a symbol of God:

> To see a World in a grain of sand,
>   And Heaven in a Wild Flower,
> Hold Infinity in the palm of your hand,
>   And Eternity in an hour.

It might be supposed that an artist setting out to illustrate the Book of Psalms would have his mind fixed on exalted things of the spirit. Yet in the Luttrell Psalter, a fine example of fourteenth-century English book illustration, the artist has painted, among the numerous decorations, interesting and amusing little scenes from English country life such as he no doubt saw going on around him. One of them shows two peasants with a plough drawn by four sturdy but far from energetic oxen. The peasant guiding the plough looks the kind of simple rustic we find in Shakespeare's plays and, later, in Thomas Hardy's works. The centuries pass and times change, but Hodge (or whatever name we give him) goes on, a permanent English type. The other man in the ploughing picture holds a long whip; the lash dangles idly over the backs of the leading pair of oxen, but the driver is paying no heed to them. He is looking back at the man behind the plough, and seems to be making some not very complimentary remark. One could quite well believe that it must have been like the back-chat between a bus driver and a conductor to-day.

'ALL OF A PIECE'

We may also be reminded that this picture, which seems curious in a religious book, is all in line with scenes in the religious plays performed in England in medieval times. Intermingled with the story of the shepherds on Christmas Eve we find passages of dialogue dealing with labour conditions, not as they were for shepherds in Palestine centuries ago but as they were for shepherds in England at the time the play was written. In other plays there are passages poking fun at local people, such as hen-pecked husbands and sheep-stealers. We know, then, that it was common for both sacred and secular themes, biblical and local ones, to be sandwiched together. If it seems incongruous and irreverent to us, it certainly was not so to our forefathers, for whom religion and everyday life went side by side. Life was much more 'all of a piece' then than it is now: a Sunday face was not different from a week-day face, nor a church-going face different from a working-face. Only in comparatively recent times has life become divided into separate compartments labelled 'Religion', 'Art', 'Work', Pleasure', and so on.

Accordingly we find art and religion and work and fun in combination in the Middle Ages, and some modern people therefore look back to that period as a Golden Age to which it would be good to return. But though life was then, for many, better balanced, less a jumble of bits of this and pieces of the other than our present-day lives are, it was also for most people a much harder life, with more disease, more dirt, more ignorance, and more cold and darkness to cope with than we have had any experience of, even in the days of coal and electricity shortages.

Though the Luttrell Psalter could only have been made

for a wealthy person or for use in church, it was evidently illuminated by an artist who had lived among peasants and observed them carefully. On that account we can take it as an example of the work of a democratic artist in close touch with the lives of ordinary people.

KINGS AND NOBLES

As we move on to the next phase in the history of English painting we find ourselves getting on to a different social level, that of the royal and titled. In the time of the English king Henry VIII the greatest painter working in England came from Germany. He was Hans Holbein. He not only made famous portraits of Henry VIII, but also carried out the wonderful series of tinted drawings of English men and women of the period which are now a priceless part of the royal collection at Windsor Castle. In his large portraits in oils, Holbein was equally successful with King Henry in magnificent Tudor costume and with the widowed young Duchess of Milan (in the National Gallery, London) wearing a black dress and standing before a very dark blue background against which her face and folded hands stand out in striking contrast. No painting could seem more serene and simple, yet none is more beautiful and unforgettable. Holbein was to English painting what Handel was long afterwards to English music: a German working in a German style who is nevertheless firmly enrolled among the artists of whom England is proud. Under the Stuarts, another foreign painter – this time of Flemish birth – Sir Anthony Van Dyck, spent some years in England producing portraits as great as Holbein's, but more brilliant and elegant and with a refinement and delicacy which shows not only the wide difference between the two painters but also the difference between the Court of Henry VIII and that of Charles I.

Van Dyck's influence has never ceased to be felt in English portraiture; that of Holbein was much more limited. Holbein was indeed so much Holbein and no one else in his larger works that it would be impossible for anyone else to paint in his style. Van Dyck's courtly style could be, and often was, imitated, though never equalled.

LITTLE PICTURES

In one direction Holbein did set a fashion in English art. Among his many accomplishments was miniature-painting. Those who illuminated manuscripts in the Middle Ages are also called miniaturists, but the word more usually means a painter of small portraits, often intended to be set in an oval or round gold mount and worn on a chain about the neck. They were sometimes done on paper, sometimes on porcelain, but often on ivory. Holbein's miniatures inspired a young man destined to become the greatest English miniaturist, Nicholas Hilliard, who belonged to Devon and began as a jeweller. His miniatures are so elaborately yet delicately painted that they have a jewel-like quality of their own. Hilliard produced tiny masterpieces of most of the great figures at the Court of Elizabeth, and the art of miniature-painting was continued by a succession of artists, of whom Isaac and Peter Oliver and Samuel Cooper were the best. Though at its finest miniature-painting is charming, it is a toy art with very limited possibilities. A collection of miniatures (there are many fine ones in the Victoria and Albert Museum, London) is less interesting than a single good specimen taken separately. That may be because a miniature has to be looked at so closely and with such concentrated attention that one soon becomes tired.

The principal Court painters to Charles II and James II, Sir Peter Lely and Sir Godfrey Kneller, had many beautiful women and handsome men for their models, and they used their opportunities to the full. These two painters should not be overlooked, for they bridged the period between Van

Dyck and Reynolds, but they are not among the greater English artists. In fact, though most of their work was done in England, they were no more Englishmen than Holbein and Van Dyck were. Lely was born in Holland and Kneller in Germany.

MIDDLE-CLASS PORTRAITS

With the passing of the Stuarts began that long period of English history in which the middle classes, at first gradually but later rapidly, displaced the aristocracy as the most influential social group. Kings no longer claimed divine right, and as they came to seem more and more like human beings and less and less like demigods, the old kind of courtier also decreased in importance. High birth and vast estates, titles and personal beauty still counted for much, but money is irresistible and merchants and traders were piling up great fortunes in the eighteenth century, as manufacturers were to do in the nineteenth century when the Industrial Revolution brought in the factory system.

From the time William III and Mary came to the throne in 1689, English portrait-painting was less centred on royalty. Most of the portraits continued to be of rich people, because only they could afford to pay the large fees required by successful artists, but as money spread increasingly over a larger part of the population, painters had different kinds of men and women among their sitters and they painted them in a more natural style. Even to-day royal portraits tend to be somewhat unnatural and flattering. Although Oliver Cromwell is said to have ordered Lely to paint him truthfully – roughness, pimples, warts, and all – not many important persons are anxious to have their blemishes advertised. If a king of Ruritania were hump-backed and cross-eyed it might be thought disloyal to paint him like that, so a make-believe version of his appearance would be adopted for official portraits, and the real person would be known to comparatively few. As late as the reign of Queen Victoria, when a lesser German artist, Winterhalter, was often employed to paint portraits of the English royal family, an artificial prettiness was popular for Court paintings.

A great artist will not paint as other people order him to, but only as he himself wants to paint. A minor artist is likely to produce flattering portraits and so to have more patrons and to make more money. It was therefore healthy for English art when painters ceased to be dependent upon the Court and were at liberty to go farther afield for their subjects. It is bad for artists to be tied by anything except an honest devotion to their work; they should not be lackeys to anyone, however powerful, in the Church, at the Court, or in the State.

PREACHER THROUGH PICTURES

The first important English painter who can be said to have been free from such control was William Hogarth. He was born poor in London in 1697, was apprenticed as a silversmith's engraver, and afterwards worked on copperplate illustrations for booksellers. He put in some part-time study at an art school; and he eloped with his master's daughter. His early portrait-paintings and caricatures of London life brought in very little money, so it was necessary for him after marriage to find a more profitable occupation. He was disgusted by the social evils of the period – immorality, drunkenness, gambling – and by all filthy habits and wasteful extravagance. Hogarth therefore set out to show up these vices in a series of moral paintings which could be copied as engravings and sold cheaply in print-shops. He hoped this might help to lessen the evils he was attacking, and at the same time bring in more money than he had been able to make previously. He succeeded in both these purposes.

Hogarth's fame in the twentieth century is due to the fact

that he was an excellent painter. In his own day and for long after he was popular and famous as a social reformer. In his moral works he was rather like a combination of Bunyan and Defoe. He preached sermons in pictures as Bunyan did in books. The scenes Hogarth drew and painted are as close to the ugly realities of a certain kind of life as anything we can find in Defoe's writings. And, like both Bunyan and Defoe, Hogarth was a good story-teller. Many English people love a good picture; most of them love a good sermon; all of them love a good story. If picture, sermon, and story are combined – as Hogarth combined them in *The Rake's Progress* and *Marriage à la Mode* – popularity is a foregone conclusion.

PICTURES-WITH-A-STORY

Hogarth's success with this part of his work was to have important consequences in English painting for a century and a half. He started a liking for story pictures (critics prefer to use the term 'narrative paintings' or 'subject pictures'), and particularly for moral story pictures. However unwilling some people may be to believe it, what really matters about a story painting is not whether it is a good story but whether it is a good painting, i.e. well designed and well painted. It is equally true that in a novel a good story is not enough. Many novels which are good stories – that is, they have plenty of action and excitement – are quickly forgotten and cease to be read because they are not well written. Bunyan's *The Pilgrim's Progress*, Defoe's *Robinson Crusoe*, and Swift's *Gulliver's Travels* are good stories, but we should not still be reading them two centuries after they were written if the authors had not also been masters of literary style – skilled in the choosing and arranging of words.

Those who followed Hogarth in narrative painting lacked his skill as a designer and colourist. (We might also say that they lacked his genius, but as genius is a quality which cannot be either described or explained it is useless to try to build any argument on it. We can recognize it when it is present, but we cannot say what it is.) Though narrative paintings remained popular with uncritical people long after Hogarth's time, such works were attacked increasingly by other picture-lovers, who carried their dislike to the extreme, insisting that all story paintings must be bad because stories belong to books and are out of place in paintings. That is not a very sensible attitude. An artist must be free to paint whatever he chooses. The goodness or the badness of a picture does not depend upon the subject, but only upon whether it is painted well or ill. To that we must add, however, that judgement, taste, and sincerity are essential to good art; and, therefore, good artists naturally do not choose 'bad', empty, or sentimental subjects. The problem of what is a 'bad' subject is a complicated and controversial one which would require a whole book to itself. It brings in a lot of other problems which doctors of divinity, doctors of philosophy, doctors of medicine, and editors of papers have strong opinions about, so we must quietly pass on to say that even the best subjects can be spoiled by bad painters.

SENTIMENT WITHOUT SENTIMENTALITY

That is why much so-called 'religious art' is unworthy of its subject and utterly contemptible as art. The aim of Christian art should be to inspire us and lift us nearer to the ideal level of Christ's teaching, not to bring Christianity down to the level of trivial human sentiment. Since the Founder of Christianity was at once divine and human, the idea of divinity should not be made secondary to humanity in imaginative portraits of Him or in pictures dealing with episodes in His life. Though the tendency in Byzantine art was to stress the divine aspect so strongly that it loses touch with humanity, it is better so than that 'religious art' of a more modern sort should encourage indulgence in uncontrolled sentiment and mere emotional sensation. Sentiment is not in itself undesirable. It is a proper and necessary ingredient in our make-up. It saves us from becoming dry and hard and cynical. But if sentiment is not kept under control it acts as an emotional drug eating into the brain, weakening the mental fibre, making us the slaves of such ignoble emotions as jealousy and envy (there are even such emotions as spiritual jealousy and spiritual envy), and finally reducing us to that flabby condition of sentimentality in which feeling tyrannizes over thinking.

The disrepute into which narrative paintings had rightly fallen by the later part of the nineteenth century was due to the fact that most of their painters chose merely sentimental anecdotes and had only small skill in composition and as colourists. In brief, their story paintings were bad because they were bad painters and poor thinkers.

Hogarth succeeded where his successors failed because (*a*) his stories were based upon realities; (*b*) he selected stories which he had thought about as well as felt about; (*c*) he therefore makes us think at least as much as we feel, and the feelings aroused in us by his paintings are not pitched monotonously on a single note, but range over anger, indignation, shame, pity, and so on; (*d*) when we know the whole of the stories by heart, we still find that his pictures *as paintings* are full of interest.

'THE RAKE'S PROGRESS'

It must have been the experience of many to find that just when they thought they had exhausted *The Rake's Progress* series as a story, the whole thing came to life anew as art. The third painting in that series is of a riotous drinking party in a crowded room where each one of more than a dozen people is actually *doing* something – drinking, talking, quarrelling, making love, stealing, changing clothes, etc.

The rake himself, drunk, is having his pockets picked by one of the disreputable women. So much is happening in the picture, there is so much bustle and apparent confusion, that we may not at first notice how cleverly the whole thing is arranged and painted. The different materials and fabrics of the suits and dresses, the drinking glasses, the wood of the furniture, the mirror and the pictures on the walls; the countenances of the men and women – all these are sources of interest. There is pleasure to be had, too, from noting the harmony of the colours – the reds and browns and blues and varying flesh-tones; and from Hogarth's grouping of the figures in a pyramidal design which is not merely geometrical but full of life and movement and variety. Someone has said that the purpose of art is to impose order on chaos, and we can see art doing that very thing in this painting by Hogarth. Upon the chaos of a drunken orgy which he shows in all its nastiness he imposes *aesthetic order* and harmony and serenity. Here an ugly subject is transformed into a beautiful painting, but without abating one jot of the *moral* ugliness of the scene.

BEAUTIFUL PAINTINGS OF UGLY THINGS

Those who have had little experience of looking at pictures and thinking about them and enjoying them, are usually at a loss to understand how anything that is not in itself a beautiful or pleasant subject can possibly become material for a beautiful work of art. They sometimes go so far as to insist that it ought not to be so. In one respect they are, of course, quite right. Although we ought not to confuse art and morality, equally we ought not to suppose that an artist would be justified in glossing over moral ugliness in order to produce a beautiful painting.

The Rake's Progress is a moral painting of immoral people, a beautiful painting of ugly people. It is a moral painting because Hogarth convinces us that a drunken orgy is an

experience we shall do well to avoid; it is a beautiful painting for the reasons (among others) suggested above, not
because the painter has made any of the persons in it *look*
beautiful. The purely aesthetic side of art depends upon
design and colour, proportion and arrangement, and so on,
none of which is in itself either moral or immoral.

LIKES AND DISLIKES

The artistic (aesthetic) side of John Smith finds certain
shapes and colours more pleasing than others; Mary Smith
is probably better pleased by a different set of shapes and
colours. Mary and John – and all the rest of us – *ought* to be
able to rule out all prejudices when dealing with aesthetic
questions, but very few people can do this. John may like a
particular shape because it reminds him of a pear; he is fond
of pears. Mary may dislike a particular shape because it
reminds her of a bomb; naturally, she hates bombs. So also
with colours. We may 'like' and 'dislike' certain colours for
reasons entirely unconnected with colour as colour. Mary
may dislike crimson because years ago she was taken ill at a
time when she was wearing a crimson frock. It would, then,
be 'natural' for Mary to dislike any picture containing crimson and any shape resembling a bomb. But if she lets herself
go on disliking a picture for reasons which have nothing to
do with art, she is shutting herself off from something which
might otherwise give her much pleasure. If she could consider the picture purely as a picture and get enjoyment from
it, she would also find herself overcoming the painful
memories left behind by the illness and the bomb. What
Mary is doing is what thousands of others do, often
with less cause – i.e. allowing prejudice born of fear to
distort her outlook and to rob her of some of life's good
things.

But it would take more persuasion than there is space for
here to clear away the many prejudices which prevent

people from enjoying art. Let us return to Hogarth's paintings.

We spoke in the first chapter of Hogarth's group portrait of *The Graham Children* (see Plate 16). It is for his portraits that he is now most praised, particularly for the portrait-heads of his servants. As an artist he was at his happiest when he was painting what we now call 'the people'. He could paint on any social level, but he came from the lower middle class and he painted people of that class and the poorer classes with understanding and affection. Homespun was his wear, not silks and lace, and he was far from despising rags. He broke away from the habit of following the Old Masters, and painted with an entirely personal vision and with absolute originality. In that sense English painting can be said to have begun with him. What is often singled out as his finest work, *The Shrimp Girl* (National Gallery, London), is little more than a sketch for a painting; yet it is fortunate that Hogarth did not elaborate it, for the picture as he left it is radiant with life. The girl seems to be bursting from the canvas, rather than painted on it by a hand which fell still and cold nearly two hundred years ago.

THE MOST SCHOLARLY PAINTER

Inexpert picture-lovers usually separate artists into two main groups: those whose work they respect and admire; and those whose work they enjoy and love. It is in the first of these groups that Sir Joshua Reynolds would be placed by the majority of laymen, since he was probably the most scholarly painter England has had. During his three years of study in Italy he filled his mind with knowledge of that country's greatest painters, and returned home convinced that such knowledge was essential to the making of a good artist. It has been supposed that Reynolds thought it was enough for a young painter to nourish his own talents on whatever he could pick up from past Italian masters, but he

was not himself a slavish imitator. Whatever he had learned
from others he absorbed and transformed into Reynolds –

> Whatever Miss T. eats,
> Turns into Miss T.

It is as impossible to imagine eighteenth-century England
without Sir Joshua Reynolds as without Dr Samuel Johnson,
but Reynolds's work, like that of Johnson, is an acquired
taste. It is easier to enjoy it in one's fifties than in one's teens.
In any balanced judgement of English art there can be
little doubt that Reynolds stands first among the portrait
painters. His mastery of rock-bottom principles has rarely if
ever been equalled in England. He painted most of the outstanding men and women of his time, while as the first
President of the Royal Academy (founded in 1768) and as a
lecturer there his influence was enormous. His *Discourses on
Art* (based on lectures delivered to Royal Academy students)
make one of the most important and most readable books on
art ever published in England. Yet, somehow, it is hard to
feel towards Reynolds anything warmer than admiration
and respect. There are moments when we are tempted to
ask if the truth about him may not be that he had everything a great painter needs except the flame of inborn
genius. That flame certainly burned brightly in his contemporary, Thomas Gainsborough, who admired and
praised Reynolds's work for its variousness. This should be
remembered as evidence that a painter sees in another
painter's work more than a non-painter can see. Gainsborough is nowadays likely to be regarded as more varied
than Reynolds, as well as fresher and more spontaneous – a
point illustrated by Plates 17 and 18. Looking at Reynolds's
portrait of *The Strawberry Girl* (Wallace Collection, London)
we may feel that the child and also the man who painted her
were on their best behaviour, and rather prim and buttoned-
up. When we turn to Gainsborough's painting of his two

daughters (National Gallery, London) we are aware of a breath of naturalness, as though we had come out of a close room into the cool open air – in spite of the fact that *The Strawberry Girl* has a landscape background while the other has not. The Gainsborough painting is in parts much less finished than Reynolds's, but it is more alive: these, we say at once, are children such as we have met a hundred times, though more real than any real children could ever be to many of us. The other, by comparison, is a learned man's mental picture of a nice child. We think of her as 'made by Reynolds' and made good but rather smug, whereas we are more inclined to think of the Gainsborough children as 'made by God' and made mischievous.

PORTRAITS IN FANCY DRESS

It was the fashion in eighteenth-century England to suppose that the clothes then worn were hardly suitable for paintings and sculpture. Statues of the statesmen often show them wearing Roman togas instead of eighteenth-century suits, and ladies preferred to be painted in fancy dress as 'Graces' and other legendary characters. Gainsborough disliked this habit. On one occasion when the husband of a society woman complained that the portrait Gainsborough had painted was not a good likeness, the artist wrote politely to say that the complaint would not have been made if she had worn ordinary clothes such as her husband was used to her wearing. The unusual costume made her look strange even to her husband's eyes. Gainsborough was a lover of naturalness because he was from his early years a lover of nature. If he could have made a living from landscapes he would have painted more of them and fewer portraits. The landscapes he did paint before he left the country for the town are among the finest English outdoor pictures; none better were done until Constable and Turner came along in the next century.

Gainsborough was born in East Anglia, at Sudbury in Suffolk, and in that district his best landscapes were painted. He was one of the most successful artists of the period and he painted numerous portraits to order. They are a glorious part of English art, but we can never cease to lament the non-existence of the other landscapes he would certainly have painted. If he could have remained in his native county, away from the dazzling artificiality of wealth and society in Bath and London, where he worked at the height of his fame, he might not have challenged Reynolds for position as the greatest English portrait-painter; but his right to be acclaimed as a greater original artist than Reynolds is suggested by one at least of his early pictures, *Robert Andrews and his Wife*, painted in Suffolk when Gainsborough was about twenty-eight. It shows a young country gentleman and his wife (and their dog) in the foreground at the left of the picture. As a portrait of the couple it is absolutely free from any trace of studio mannerism or artificiality. They are as natural as the tree beneath which Mrs Andrews sits on a garden bench with her husband standing beside her. It is an excellent double portrait. But that is not all. The rest of the picture is as lovely a landscape as was ever painted, enchantingly fresh and natural – a piece of Suffolk transferred to canvas. Gainsborough was fond of blue (*The Blue Boy*, one of his most famous works, was sold to America for a fortune years ago), but he never used that colour more deliciously than for Mrs Andrews's pale blue pannier dress. To describe it as 'pale blue' is ridiculously insufficient. Mr Sacheverell Sitwell (who calls this 'the most beautiful painting ever done by an Englishman') has likened the colour to 'blue spray on one day in ten years in the Baltic or Northern Seas'. Or 'perhaps it is the blue of a fresh water lake, where the ripples have slight blue crests. . . . ' In this picture we have the pure poetry of painting, which is so rare and precious that nothing done by Reynolds, nor by Gainsborough in later life, can compete with it.

The first half of the nineteenth century was the great age of English landscape painters, following after Gainsborough and John Crome, the founder of the Norwich School. The last years of the eighteenth century had also seen the rise of a group of water-colour painters (Cozens, Girtin, Cox, and others) whose works are among the most 'Englishy' things that can be found in all English art. Girtin also greatly influenced Turner who, with Constable, can conveniently be dealt with in the next chapter.

AGAINST 'ARTIFICIAL PAINTING'

In 1848, William Holman-Hunt, Dante Gabriel Rossetti, John Everett Millais, and a few lesser artists and writers banded themselves together to form a group named the Pre-Raphaelite Brotherhood. Their aim was to free paintings from the artificial mannerisms which, so they considered, had become increasingly attached to them since the time of Raphael in early-sixteenth-century Italy. Pre-Raphaelite pictures had a strong religious bent, particularly those of Holman-Hunt, whose *The Light of the World* (at Keble College, Oxford) became the most popular picture of its kind in nineteenth-century England. Rossetti's work had a marked literary flavour due to his interest in Dante, the Italian poet, and in the Bible and the Arthurian legends. Millais – who later became a very popular and successful artist, a knight, and President of the Royal Academy – painted, about 1850, *Christ in the Carpenter's Shop*, probably the best of the Pre-Raphaelite pictures. It was at first bitterly attacked by religious people and in the papers. They disliked the artist's careful attention to naturalistic detail and thought it was irreverent to represent the Holy Family as ordinary people in an ordinary workshop with ordinary carpenter's tools and ordinary planks and shavings.

It was a rule of the Pre-Raphaelites, before their short-lived Brotherhood broke up, to paint everything from actual models and not from memory or from studio properties. Sometimes they could not carry out this rule to the last letter, and it said that Millais, being unable to find a flock of sheep to paint in the sheepfold which is seen through the door of the carpenter's shop, had to content himself with buying a sheep's head! This care for detail, which started from a desire for truth and absolute sincerity, afterwards became a fad and lingered far past the time when photography had sounded the death-knell of that kind of painting.

Before the camera was invented, painters were required much oftener than they are now to make what we call documentary paintings, i.e. pictures intended to do little more than record the actual physical appearances of persons and places. While that was necessary, the closer the artist kept to plain facts the more accurate and useful were his paintings as a record. Many of Turner's early pictures were topographical; that is, they faithfully represented details of the features of the places painted. When photography came in, most of the reasons for realistic painting went out. Unless a painter could do more than a camera could do he was no longer worth his keep, since a photographer charges only about as many shillings (or perhaps pence) as a painter charges guineas. It is true that moneyed people continued to expect paintings to be hardly more than coloured photographs, but younger artists were becoming dissatisfied with their position as expensive supplementary photographers and copyists of Nature. This dissatisfaction helped (though it was not entirely responsible for) the revolution which, as the nineteenth century closed, introduced non-representational or abstract painting, of which we are to talk in our final chapter.

8

Modern Paintings

THIS chapter is to deal mainly with 'modern' painters, i.e. those of the last half-century or so, but it would be misleading to attempt to fix a date for the beginnings of 'modern' art, since its roots go deep down into the past. Some works of art which appear to be new in style may on examination turn out to be very old. Perhaps the most startling instance of this in our time is to be found in the sculptures of Jacob Epstein, much of whose work has been resented and attacked by those who thought it ugly and brutal because it was strange to them. Since the revival of interest in ancient classical art in the sixteenth century, nearly all European sculpture has followed the Greek style and we have become so used to that style that anything different tends to look 'wrong' to most of us. Epstein is a highly original artist, and in the opinion of many well-informed critics he is the greatest sculptor ever to have worked in England. We need not accept that opinion, but before we disagree with it we must have some firm ground for any contrary opinion. If we are to understand Epstein's style and not merely to condemn it because we are prejudiced, we must look far back into the past to the sculptures of such un-Greek people as the ancient Assyrians, to whom he is closer in spirit than he is to the Greeks. We may ourselves much prefer Greek art to Assyrian, but no modern artist can reasonably be condemned for having preferences different from ours, or for looking backward to a time and place which does not much attract us (or about which we know nothing). Sculpture is not our concern here, but what has been said of Epstein can also be applied in principle to present-day painting, though its ancestry is quite different. Before we venture to attack anything 'modern' it is advisable to find out what its roots were. They may be very old and very respectable instead of new and (as some people would think) disreputable.

This is not the place, however, for so big an undertaking as to inquire into the ancestry of everything that seems new in modern painting. We must be content to glance at a few earlier painters whose work has influenced, sometimes more, sometimes less, the artists of our own time.

A PAINTER OF EVERYDAY THINGS

With the first to be mentioned, the French painter Chardin, who worked in the middle of the eighteenth century, it is not so much a question of considering whether he has or has not influenced modern painters, as of taking note of resemblances between his outlook and interests and ours. In date, Chardin comes between Watteau and Fragonard, who excelled in depicting the artificial life and romantic daydreams of the aristocracy (see pp. 114–15), but Chardin turned his attention to ordinary people and simple things, particularly to kitchen utensils and plain eatables such as loaves of bread and joints of meat. This 'still-life' (as it is called) can be dull and boring, as it is in the works of certain minor seventeenth-century Dutch painters who produced pictures of dead game and poultry, though the great Vermeer in *The Cook* and other paintings shows how intensely interesting and even fascinating common everyday objects can be. Vermeer had masterly skill in suggesting to our eyes, and through our eyes to our tactile sense, the differing textures of various materials and substances. Chardin seems to go further, making inanimate substances interesting *in themselves*, not only interesting because they are part of a pictorial composition. A Chardin still-life may well remind us of lines in Rupert Brooke's poem *The Great Lover*, in which he speaks of his affection for 'white plates and cups ... the strong crust of friendly bread ... the cool kindliness of sheets ...

blankets; grainy wood . . . hot water . . . furs . . . old clothes', and so on.

It is not, however, because of this (what we might call) romance-of-the-commonplace quality in Chardin that he now and again reminds us of the much later painter Cézanne (who did his utmost to keep any kind of sentiment out of his work), but because Chardin went to great pains to simplify the design of his pictures and to get rid of everything but bare essentials. He would make several attempts at painting the same group of objects until, in the final version, he had satisfied himself that only what was absolutely necessary was left in. In that respect he was very much like a number of twentieth-century artists who aim at what has been called 'stripped design' – i.e. getting down to the bones of art and not being content with its pretty outside. But there is more than that in Chardin. If he gives us the bones he also gives us the soul. Our first impulse on seeing a still-life by him is to exclaim 'How *real* that looks!' 'Reality' in his pictures is more internal than external – reality of substance more than reality of surface. Just as a good portrait-painter *sees into* the character of the person he paints, so Chardin seemed to see into the nature of the loaf he was painting and he makes us sensible of the *virtue* of bread (Plate 21).[1] Cézanne, about 150 years afterwards, worked out a system by means of which, in landscape, still-life (Plate 22), portraits, etc., he was able to emphasize internal structure more than external appearances. (You will find something more about that on page 168.)

THE INNOCENT EYE

Many artists take pleasure in painting elaborate and complex pictures which look so difficult to do that the painters

[1]. Plate 21, though signed 'Chardin 1754', may in fact be by an imitator; but even if that is so, it closely illustrates Chardin's simplicity and also shows how strong his influence must have been.

get credit for cleverness. The newer kind of artist in recent times has taken the opposite road: he goes to as great pains to simplify as his grandfathers did to complicate. He simplifies to such an extent that to many eyes the result may appear as crude and untaught as a child's drawing, and is condemned on that account by those who say scornfully 'Anyone could do that!' It is, in fact, far harder than it looks to draw and paint like a child when one isn't a child, because it is much harder to unlearn than to learn. It is still harder to recover the 'innocent eye' of a child when one is grown up and one's whole outlook has become changed by education and experience – become, as we say, sophisticated. Much that is apparently crude in twentieth-century painting is due to a conviction among artists that our tired and too-clever world needs to see life afresh through a child-like innocence of vision.

There is nothing crude about Chardin's paintings. He was a very skilful, accomplished, and 'finished' painter. But in spite of the unlimited care and attention that he gave to his work, the result always looked as if it were the spontaneous product of his innocence of eye.

Whatever extraordinary qualities there may be in Chardin's pictures when we consider them carefully, they look quite ordinary at a casual glance. They do not startle, as many 'modern' paintings do. Indeed, so many of these are arrestingly different from what older people became accustomed to in an earlier generation, that it is usual to emphasize the difference by labelling them 'modernistic' instead of just 'modern'. Most of the later works to be discussed in the rest of this chapter and in the next chapter have at some time and by someone been put into the modernistic class. At first, all of them looked strange; a number do so still; and all of them have been scoffed at, often by people who have afterwards completely changed their opinion of the pictures that at first offended them. It may save a lot of silly jeering if we realize that when a work of art makes us angry it may actually only be causing us aesthetic growing-pains: our taste and powers of appreciation may be undergoing a rather painful stretching and enlargening process which will be to our advantage afterwards and open up new sources of understanding and enjoyment.

LABELS

One difference between painting during the last hundred years and painting in earlier times is that theories have latterly been given more prominence, and artists have been readier to join 'movements' and to form groups for the purpose of carrying on and encouraging a particular kind or style of painting. Centuries ago, although certain artists were no doubt aware that they wanted to paint differently from others, there were no newspapers to bring their ideas to the attention of the public. If there had been, we might now be calling the Florentine School the 'Scientific Movement in Painting'. But artists were then labelled according to birthplace or workplace not according to the theories, if any, that underlay their pictures.

In the past century or so we have had the Pre-Raphaelite Brotherhood (see pp. 135–6), the Romantic Movement, the Realistic Movement, the Impressionist Movement, the Post-Impressionist Movement, the *Fauvres* ('wild men'), the Cubists, the Futurists, the Neo-Primitives, the Surrealist Movement, and others of less interest. In England in the 1880s the New English Art Club was started by painters sympathetic to the Impressionists who were then active in France. The N.E.A.C. was helpful in encouraging young English artists cold-shouldered by the conservative Royal Academy, which does not readily admit the newer kinds of painting to its annual exhibition. The French Impressionists had had a similar experience in their country, where, being constantly excluded by the Salon in Paris (the equivalent of the annual exhibition of new paintings at the Royal

Academy in London), they started their own exhibition and quickly became the most important group in France.

MELTING THE ICE

Earlier, there was the French Romantic Movement, dating from the 1830s. This was linked particularly with Eugène Delacroix, who became the first to break away from the cold lifelessness of Napoleon's official painter, Jacques Louis David. Delacroix's *Liberty Leading the People* shows the symbolic figure of France waving the tricolour at the head of a company of armed civilians fighting on the barricades for the Republican cause. The modern spirit and fire of Delacroix melted away the mock-classical ice of David and brought French painting into touch with the life of the period. Honoré Daumier, ten years younger than Delacroix, and Gustave Courbet, eleven years younger still, went much farther in that direction. They threw over Delacroix's poetry and heroics and, Honoré Daumier especially, found their subjects in the lives of the common people. It was of Courbet's work that the word 'realistic' was first used to describe paintings, though there is more true realism in Daumier's pictures of aspects of life in Paris and in Jean François Millet's of the lives of the peasants in the fields. 'Realism' is, however, a word often used too narrowly. There is no sound reason for confining it, as is usually done, to (*a*) pictures of (or books about) the poor and depressed classes; (*b*) pictures and books dealing with the sordid underside of upper-class life. Any truthful presentation of life, high or low, pleasant or ugly, is entitled to be called realistic; so also is a faithful landscape painting. It is perhaps a little confusing that, in relation to works of art, 'realistic' sometimes means that the artist has selected an unromantic subject, and sometimes that he has painted (any subject) photographically. But the term 'Realistic Movement' usually refers to choice of subject. For work which is photographic in style the term 'representational painting' (see page 162) is frequently used.

*

'SNAPSHOT' PAINTINGS

The Impressionist Movement, which stirred many Frenchmen to fury in the 1870s and after, was a studied attempt to apply to painting the results of careful scientific inquiry into the nature of light. Most landscape artists before then had painted as though light were constant. The Impressionists, knowing that light changes from moment to moment throughout the day and that colour cannot exist apart from light, came to the conclusion that a landscape painting could be true to Nature only if it gave an instantaneous *impression* of a scene as it appeared at a single moment in time. In effect, to borrow the language of amateur photographers, the Impressionists thought snapshots were closer to Nature, more realistic or naturalistic, than time-exposures. At a given moment the sunshine may be sparkling on a shiny leaf, or on a smooth stone, or on a brook. At the next moment the earth has moved and perhaps a cloud has come between the sun and the earth: then the sparkle has gone and the light has become duller and flatter. Since the earth never ceases changing its position in relation to the sun, no scene looks exactly alike at any two consecutive moments. If a landscape painter intends to get really close to the actual appearance of the bit of country he is painting, he must choose a particular moment and try to get on to his canvas an exact impression of what the scene was like at that single moment. For conveying an impression of the continually changing quality and strength of light the sparkles on leaf and stone, on water and wet earth, are very important.

Yet how can paint be made to seem to sparkle and give the vibrating and shimmering effect that light actually has out of doors on a bright day?

A painter usually mixes colours on his palette; but though

the mixing of yellow and blue gives him green, some of the 'life' that was in the unmixed pigments is lost from the blended colour which he brushes on to the canvas. If, instead, he puts direct into the picture a small dab of pure unmixed yellow side by side with another dab of pure unmixed blue, and then repeats the dabs of yellow and blue side by side until he has a group of them, the eyes of the spectator looking at the picture blend them as the result of an optical illusion. If he stands at the right distance, he does not see separate dabs of yellow and blue; he gets the impression of seeing a patch of green, and the colour has a live and sparkling appearance. This was not altogether an original discovery of the Impressionists, for earlier landscape-painters had taken advantage of this optical illusion, though they had not studied the whole matter scientifically as the Impressionists did. Furthermore, the Impressionists, when they had worked out their theories, made up their minds that they would use only the colours of the spectrum – red, orange, yellow, green, blue, indigo, violet – and have nothing to do with the darker earthy colours. They also made a special study of shadows and found that there are subtle colour-combinations in shadows and that these should be painted as arrangements of colour, not merely as dark patches. The Impressionists' determination to avoid all but the colours of the spectrum explains a term which frequently appears in writings about them: they are described as having painted with a 'spectral palette'.

CONSTABLE BROUGHT LIGHT INTO PAINTINGS

When English painters who had studied in Paris brought Impressionism into England, they were angrily rebuked for following what was regarded as an outlandish foreign fashion which would never do for English homes and galleries. Nothing could illustrate more plainly than this what was said a few pages back: namely, that it is unwise to condemn what seems 'new' before finding out whether it may not be a reappearance of something old which was accepted and praised before. If late-nineteenth-century English art-lovers who attacked Impressionism as 'a foreign fad' had been asked whether they liked John Constable's and J. M. W. Turner's paintings, most of them would no doubt have answered with an abrupt 'Yes!', implying that it was a stupidly unnecessary question. If they had then been told that French Impressionism had its roots in the landscapes of Constable and Turner they would probably have snapped back, even more abruptly, 'Nonsense!' Yet it was so.

In 1824 certain paintings by Constable were sent across the Channel to be exhibited in Paris. There they were seen by French artists (of an older generation than the Impressionists), upon whom the influence of Constable began to work, though at first in only a slight degree. About fifty years later, during the Franco-Prussian war of 1870, several of the younger French painters took refuge in England. Having seen Constable's and Turner's pictures, they went back to France after the war like men who had seen a great light. It was then that the Impressionist Movement was born.

What they had found in the English pictures was a new attitude towards Nature and a new way of dealing with light in painting. While it is true that Gainsborough's early landscapes were the work of a young man who loved the country and painted what he saw for himself out of doors, the growth of his practice as a fashionable portrait-painter meant that he had less and less time to spend in the country. The landscapes he then painted occasionally for his own pleasure were done chiefly from memory inside his studio in Bath and later in London, and however magnificent they were they had lost the freshness which gave such simple loveliness to the earlier ones. Unlike Gainsborough, Constable would not turn away from landscape-painting as the proper work of his life, even when he found that no one would buy his pictures. However neglected, however poor, he kept on.

At that time art-collectors thought that painters ought to paint in such a way that their pictures would resemble those of the Old Masters, which were subdued in colour and had a mellow browny autumn tone. In order to protect the surface from dirt, oil paintings must be varnished. After a while the varnish itself becomes dirty and discoloured, with the consequence that the original colours appear changed and the whole picture is dimmed and develops the brown tone which was mistakenly supposed to have been intended by the painters. It is not until the dirty varnish is removed and clean varnish substituted that we can see the painter's own colours. In the nineteenth century fresh and brilliant colours were so much disliked that yellow instead of clear varnish was often used with the purpose of 'toning down' the picture. Some artists actually used dull colours, mistakenly supposing that the Old Masters had themselves painted brownish pictures. When the National Gallery in London exhibited its recently cleaned paintings in 1947 many people were shocked, but more were delighted to find that the Old Masters loved brilliant colours as much as we ourselves do.

Constable quite rightly refused to paint 'brown' landscapes. He not only kept to Nature's own colours, he also did his utmost to get into his paintings as much as he possibly could of the element that makes Nature's colours, i.e. Light (Plate 20). He had a wonderful gift for that, and he used it even when he was painting more or less in the traditional manner, but he was one of the first to make a point of using in certain parts of his pictures those dabs of thick paint which reflect light at various angles, as a coloured stone with a number of facets does in a more obvious manner. The French painters afterwards called Impressionists were fascinated by the vibrating quality of light which Constable got into his landscapes, and they began enthusiastically to develop the idea.

TURNER'S VISIONS OF COLOUR

They received another shock of delighted surprise from Turner's works. Turner had begun by producing scores of very beautiful paintings (many in water-colour) of the numerous scenes and places he visited for that purpose in Great Britain and on the Continent. He continued to be a great traveller. The outstanding feature of his work then was, as Ruskin never tired of pointing out, 'truth to Nature'. He seemed to know, complete from A to Z, not only the exact appearance of everything in Nature, but also how everything was formed and constructed – each leaf, each twig, each branch, each tree. . . . He was not a niggling artist, however: he did not concentrate excessively on detail and so lose the effect of the whole. It may be that, at length, Turner exhausted his interest in that kind of painting because before he was 30 he could do it so well. Whatever the reason, by the age of 50 (he lived until 1851, when he was 76) he was painting those amazingly and at times riotously colourful pictures which are more widely known than his other works. No one has come closer than Turner to painting pure light breaking up into its prismatic colours. He painted mist, spray, rain, steam, cloud, so that solid objects seen dimly would appear insubstantial and dream-like and as though dissolving in the light-and-colour-drenched atmosphere. When we have looked at it many times we may come round to thinking that the most beautiful picture Turner ever painted in this manner is the *Interior at Petworth* (National Gallery, London – Plate 23) where a large and solid indoor apartment seems almost like a gossamer veil bathed in a glory of luminous colour. This picture may bother us at first, if we try to puzzle out the contents of the room, but if we are content to enjoy it as a wonderful vision of light and colour we shall find it completely satisfying.

There can be no doubt that Turner was a very great painter, but it often happens that great men have a bad influence. Golden visions in painting are all very well, but we live in a solid world and solidity is the necessary foundation for art as well as for most other things. We can fly towards the sun in an aircraft but sooner or later the machine has to come back to earth, and all the time it has to be kept under control to prevent it from falling to destruction. An artist's imagination is rather like that. He can soar far away from solidity and the world of real things but he cannot soar for ever, and unless he keeps his imagination under control it will destroy itself. Unlike the aircraft it will not crash back to earth, however, it will break up like a bursting star and become nothing but a bright haze of meteoric dust.

TOO MANY RAINBOWS

The greatest artists never carry a theory to extremes: nor do they ever allow themselves to become the victims of uncontrolled imagination. It was Claude Monet who carried the Impressionist experiment to the farthest point by trying to paint light in an almost pure state. When an artist attempts to do that, his paintings tend to become hazy and vague for want of the solid substance and structure required to provide the reflecting surface which is necessary to make light visible as colour. Even a rainbow must have a screen of water-vapour to make it visible; and though we all run to see a rainbow we only do so because rainbows are rare. If we could see them every day we should find them sickly and gaudy, and turn our eyes away in distaste. Too much Impressionism of the extremer sort would soon become as tiresome as too many rainbows and too many cream fondants. No lover of paintings can be other than glad and grateful to the Impressionists for reminding a drab world of the glory and wonder of light and colour, but painting had to come back to earth. Monet did some of his pictures in series, showing the same scene several times in varying conditions of light. At one time he chose a lily pond; at another, the front of a cathedral. So much was he carried away by the desire to make light and colour independent of solid matter that the cathedral appears more immaterial than the pond.

An earlier French painter, Corot, one of the finest nineteenth-century pre-Impressionists, produced a large number of beautifully firm landscapes before he turned to the painting of scenes in which a mist-laden atmosphere envelops everything in a filmy silvery-grey veil. The effect is cloyingly sentimental. On the other hand, Whistler, the American painter who settled in England after studying in Paris, made twilight and evening and morning mists on the Thames memorably lovely without a trace of sentimentality.

Though I have singled out Claude Monet from among the French Impressionists for special comment, this is not because he was the best of the group, but only because his paintings illustrate most clearly the dangers of carrying an excellent idea too far. All roads lead us back sooner or later to the ancient Greek ideal of balance. Enough is better than a feast.

EVERYTHING IS GOOD TO PAINT

As we now look back upon the Impressionists from a distance in time, it is Edouard Manet who stands out from all the others. He was so much a master of the art and craft of painting that everything he did was effortless, and it is difficult to say more about his paintings than one can say about a miracle – 'It has happened!' It is far easier to recognize that Manet's *Le Bar aux Folies-Bergère* (Plate 26) is a great painting than to say why it is great – and one's awareness of its beauty grows with better acquaintance. But *why?* The barmaid is far from pretty; and, after all, it is not she that claims our closest attention. She does not really contribute more to our enjoyment of the picture than do the wine and beer and liqueur bottles, and the bowl of fruit, and the two flowers in the glass. We go on to ask why a painting of an ordinary labelled beer bottle should thrill anyone? The answer no doubt is that Manet loved painting for painting's sake so much that the commonest things became uncommon:

> He nothing common did or mean
> Upon that memorable scene. . . .

If a painter has a wife whom he loves very much his love for her does not guarantee that if he paints her portrait it will be a masterpiece. It will not be a masterpiece unless he is a great painter. And if he *is* a great painter, whether he loves his wife or not will make very little difference to the quality and merit of his portrait of her. A great painter's portrait of his worst enemy can be as good a painting as if it were a portrait of his best friend. So, to Manet, everything was good to paint, whether it was a beer-bottle or a beautiful woman. Painting was his supreme enjoyment, and as he had enough money from other sources to make him independent he could paint whatever interested him, with no need to bother about whether anyone would buy his pictures.

THE JOY OF LIVING

Yet however much the joy of painting runs through Manet's works they do not express any obvious joy of life. In that respect they are reserved, almost austere. Pierre Renoir's paintings, on the other hand, sing with the joy of living; sometimes they shout aloud. This sense of joy is the very soul of his pictures, whether their subject be still-life, landscape, a crowd beneath umbrellas in the rain, portraits of children, or girls bathing. Towards the end of his long life he suffered from partial paralysis of the hands and had to paint with the brushes tied to his fingers. This aggravated his tendency (seen to some extent in his earlier pictures) to paint fleshy and bloated forms in feverishly, hot colours. At his best, however, he gave a pearly loveliness to the tones and texture of the human skin, while the colours in all his mature works have a summery peach-like ripeness. Renoir's paintings need no signature. They have a distinctive bloom which is unmistakable, whatever their subject.

PICTURES FULL OF LIFE AND MOVEMENT

In England the most popular of the French Impressionists is probably Edgard Degas. This is due to the widespread liking for ballet, of which Degas painted a number of pictures. He would not have been very pleased to know that his works were enjoyed mainly for their subject-matter for, like most of the Impressionists, he was much more interested in problems of painting – technical problems – than in choosing popular subjects. He seems often to have preferred unattractive ones, for those have the advantage of causing spectators to think chiefly about the painting itself, instead of about what it is a painting of. Degas usually painted people when they were engaged in some form of work, not merely posing for a picture: dancers rehearsing, laundresses ironing, milliners trimming hats, women washing themselves, horses and jockeys on the racecourse. Remarkably few of the women in his pictures are even moderately good-looking. There is so much life and movement in Degas's works that we might suppose he painted them quickly and direct from the models, putting down what was before his eyes at the moment. Actually he preferred to paint in his studio from rough notes made beforehand – except that at one period he had a bath fitted up in the studio so that he could observe the natural movements of a model drying her hair or stepping in and out of the bath. He was a very studious and deliberate artist, not an impulsive or spontaneous one.

Although his popularity comes in part from the fact that ballet now attracts millions of people, those who like Degas's pictures for that reason can hardly fail to enjoy, also, his glorious colours. He very frequently used pastels, which have one advantage over oil-paints, water-colours, tempera, fresco, etc. – they are not mixed with any liquid medium but are applied as solid colour. This means that the tones are not lowered and that the colours of the finished picture can be flashingly brilliant. Degas's pastels gleam and glow with the sheen of rich satins. It is this emphasis on colour which makes us include him with the Impressionists, though he quickly branched off on a line entirely his own.

JAPANESE ART COMES IN

Like Manet and other painters at that time, Degas was influenced, at least temporarily, by the Japanese colour-prints which merchants were then importing into Europe from the Far East. In Japanese pictures distance is represented more by the careful placing of objects in the picture-space (*spatial relations*, see pp. 86–7) than by perspective in the Western style, and there is little attempt to indicate roundness and bulk and solidity by modelling and shading. Much Chinese art is like that, too, and if you have a piece of willow-pattern ware in the house you can see just what Charles Lamb meant in his essay on *Old China* when he wrote of 'that world before perspective – a china tea-cup':

Here is a young and courtly Mandarin, handing tea to a lady from a salver – two miles off. See how distance seems to set off respect! And here the same lady, or another – for likeness is identity on tea-cups – is stepping into a little fairy boat, moored on the hither side of this calm garden river, with a dainty mincing foot, which in a right angle of incidence (as angles go in our world) must infallibly land her in the midst of a flowery mead – a furlong off on the other side of the same strange stream!

There are fewer quaintnesses in a Japanese colour-print than on a Chinese tea-cup, and neither Degas nor any other of the Impressionists and their followers imitated this oriental style very closely. They took what they wanted, but no more. Degas moved far away from the Japanese style, and went to infinite trouble to build up the figures of his bathing women until they seem to be sculptured in colour rather than painted in only two dimensions on a flat surface.

Manet, Van Gogh, and Gauguin were among the other late-nineteenth-century painters influenced by the style of Japanese colour-prints, but it is in Whistler's pictures that the influence can be most plainly seen. The way in which a foreign style may be adapted by an artist for his own different purpose is shown in a particularly interesting way in Whistler's portrait of his mother (in The Louvre, Paris) and in his portrait of Thomas Carlyle (Glasgow Art Gallery). Both of these are painted mainly as arrangements of subdued flat colour after the Japanese style, yet both are excellent as portraits, the one of a stern old American lady, the other of a rugged old Scots philosopher.

9

More Modern Paintings

LIVES of painters are not often especially interesting apart from their work. This was not so, however, with Vincent Van Gogh and Paul Gauguin, two Post-Impressionists whose tragic stories ran together for a while. Neither of them began to paint until after he reached manhood; yet, to both, painting was to become a consuming passion.

Paul Gauguin, born in Paris in 1848, had some South American blood in his veins. In his 'teens he went to sea, but settled six years later as a stockbroker in Paris, married, made money, and seemed well on the way to becoming rooted as the prosperous head of a middle-class family. Then he took up painting as a hobby and began to pass his spare time with the Impressionists in cafés and on holidays in the country. At first his amateur paintings were conventional in style, but they became increasingly strange as Gauguin dug deeper into the possibilities of this passion for art which was to wreck his successful business life. At the age of 35 he made up his mind to leave stockbroking altogether and become a professional painter. That meant financial disaster for himself and his wife and five children, for no one would buy his pictures. Soon his wife went back to her family in Denmark, while Gauguin almost starved in Paris. After a season in Brittany he went to Panama and worked as a labourer in the canal zone until he had made enough money to take him to the tropical island of Martinique. Illness and the unfriendly climate compelled him to work his passage back to France, where he managed to sell in Paris a few of the paintings he had made abroad. About that time he met Van Gogh and in the later part of 1888 went to live with him at Arles, in Provence. As we shall see later, their association ended in calamity, and in the spring of 1891 Gauguin sailed for the South Seas and passed the remaining twelve years of his life among the islanders there, except for one unhappy return visit to Europe. From the time he first took to painting until the time he died, solitary and destitute, in a native hut on the island of Hiva-Oa in the Marquesas group, Gauguin had twenty years of what would be complete misery to most of us. Yet during those years he painted a seemingly endless succession of pictures which, in their unique way, are among the finest works produced during the last hundred years.

Gauguin soon abandoned the Impressionist method and developed a style unlike any other before or since. There are, at times, faint traces of the Byzantine manner, and sometimes of the Dutch, of primitive Negro art, of the Japanese colour-prints, and of other styles, in the pictures painted before his contact with the Tahitians and Marquesans brought all these into a single focus. He had 'found himself' at last.

IN THE SOUTH SEAS

Whatever sufferings and privations and sordid degradations Gauguin plunged through, he developed into a genius and painted with almost demoniac frenzy in the islands; painted on rough sacking if no other material was at hand. When we first see these later paintings – of native people, tropical landscapes, etc. – they may shock our eyes with their riotously violent contrasts of colour. But if, to begin with, they remind us of a startlingly bright patchwork quilt, before long their strangeness ceases to be disturbing. Their tropical atmosphere seeps into us; we no longer dislike them for their unlikeness to other paintings; and we recognize their wonderful decorative qualities. Gauguin hated the artificialities and restraints of modern European civilization, and as a painter he saw with an uncivilized and un-European eye. He therefore felt no urge to paint in a traditional European manner.

He obeyed only his own eye and his own imagination in regard to form, design, and the use of colour-contrasts instead of graduated harmonies of colour. One of his finest and most famous pictures is a Madonna and Child (called *Ia Orana Maria*) in which the biblical characters are represented as South Sea islanders in a jungle clearing. However startling this may seem, we recall that the Italians, the Flemings, the Dutch, the French, the Spanish, all transported Mary and the Christ Child into the painter's own local environment and represented them as Europeans of the painter's own nationality. It is therefore no more strange to transport them to the South Seas and to represent them as native people. *Ia Orana Maria* is at once realistic and reverent, and has more true spiritual force than many of the conventional Madonnas which are accepted without question as 'religious art'.

A PAINTER AMONG THE POOR

Vincent Van Gogh was born in 1853 at Zundert, a small town in Holland close to the Belgian border. His father was a clergyman and it was intended that Vincent should prepare himself for the same vocation. He had a strong religious strain and intense sympathy for poor and suffering people, but was unfitted for close and regular study. His uncle managed an art gallery at The Hague, and Vincent began work there when he was 17. Three years later he was sent to the London branch of the business as a clerk. While in England, where for a time he became a school teacher, he fell in love with his landlady's daughter. She did not return his affection, and his intensely melancholy nature was further troubled and saddened by this. Returning home, he took up work a few years later as a lay missionary in the Borinage, a coal-mining district of Belgium, sharing the poverty and hunger and misery in which the inhabitants existed. This bitter experience convinced Van Gogh that his duty was not simply to preach to these unhappy people but to live among them as one of themselves.

Though it was not until he was 30 that he started to paint, he began to make drawings some years before, and found this a consoling pastime while he was living in almost complete beggary among the miners to whom he gave everything he possessed, going hungry and in rags himself. He even gave away his bed.

His younger brother, Theo, employed in the Paris headquarters of the art business, sent what little money he could spare, and this enabled Vincent to tramp about, visiting cities where he could take lessons in drawing and painting. After another unhappy love affair and a year spent in trying to save a worthless woman, he took to living and painting among the Dutch peasants. Then came a winter in Antwerp (during which he developed a strong liking for Rubens's paintings and also for Japanese art), followed by two years in Paris. There he and Theo lived together in the artists' quarter at Montmartre, and Vincent fell under the spell of the Impressionists, in whose fashion he painted for a while. Theo supplied him with the necessary artist's materials and accepted finished pictures in exchange.

DRENCHED WITH SUNSHINE

Early in 1880, disgusted and tired of Paris, Vincent suddenly went south to Arles and soaked himself in the burning Provençal sunshine. There he painted, painted, painted. Never before in the history of art had there been paintings so drenched with sunlight. He painted not only landscapes in the country round about Arles, but also town scenes, cafés, flowers (especially sunflowers), fruit trees, portraits of ordinary people such as the local postman, and his own small simple bedroom; and when he went for a trip to the Mediterranean coast he made paintings of boats at the edge of the sea. By that time he had left the Impressionist style behind him. The sun seems to have scorched away almost everything he had ever taken from other artists and left only what was entirely his own. Perhaps the one exception was that he kept his liking for the simple patterns of Japanese prints with their areas of flat colour.

The painting of his bedroom at Arles is among his best-known works, and many people who have at first thought it ugly and its chairs, table, and wooden bedstead badly drawn, find themselves becoming very fond of it and unable any longer to see it as a picture full of odd angles. They are then forced to ask themselves why, at first, their own eyes saw oddly. The answer is that whereas, before, they had known only one way of painting and had become used to the old familiar kind of perspective, they have now learned through Van Gogh's eyes that there are other ways of seeing, and of painting what is seen. So we come back to the words quoted from Blake on page 15: 'A fool sees not the same tree that a wise man sees.' We could go further and say: 'No man sees exactly the same tree (or chair, or bed) that another man sees.' We all have our own particular way of seeing, just as we all have our own particular way of speaking, walking, and so on. Van Gogh saw differently from most other people, but we are not therefore entitled to say that his way of seeing was wrong. It was one of the many ways of seeing that are possible for human eyes.

Van Gogh was an excellent letter-writer as well as a great painter, and we are fortunate in having his description of the bedroom picture, for it helps us to know how one of his works was regarded by himself:

... This time it's just simply my bedroom, only here colour is to do everything ... is to be suggestive here of *rest* or of sleep in general. In a word, to look at the picture ought to rest the brain or rather the imagination.

The walls are pale violet. The ground is of red tiles.

The wood of the bed and chairs is the yellow of fresh butter, the sheets and pillows very light greenish lemon.

The coverlet scarlet. The window green.

The toilet table orange, the basin blue.

The doors lilac.

And that is all – there is nothing in this room with closed shutters.

The broad lines of the furniture again must express inviolable rest. Portraits on the walls, and a mirror and a towel and some clothes.

The frame – as there is no white in the picture – will be white. . . .

. . . you see how simple the conception is. The shadows and the shadows thrown are suppressed, it is painted in free flat washes like the Japanese prints.[1]

Violet, red, yellow, green, orange, blue, lilac. . . . Here, in areas of pure unmixed colour, is almost the whole range of the spectrum. The most obvious difference between the later works of Van Gogh and those of the Impressionist Monet is that whereas Monet put on his colours in little dabs and strokes so that the spectator's eye would blend them, Van Gogh often spread thick paint over broad areas of the picture and made no attempt to even-out or smooth the surface. The picture sometimes appears to be modelled in paint, for the colour is left rough and craggy, standing up in relief with hundreds of facets which reflect light in all directions and also cast tiny shadows where crests of paint overhang slightly like miniature waves. The effect is dazzling and exciting, for it must be remembered that these innumerable gleams and minute shadows play over a surface of pure primary colour.

SEEN WITHOUT PREJUDICE

Our eyes have become so accustomed to seeing the pictures of the older Masters through a film of dirty varnish which tones down the original colours, that the vivid works of

1. Letter 554 to Theo (*Further Letters of Vincent Van Gogh 1886–99*), written just before Gauguin's arrival in Arles.

modern Masters are startling – and many people are still shocked by them. But unless we are stubbornly determined to cling to our prejudices, we soon become unshocked and begin to enjoy the tonic effect of paintings which light up any room they are in and also lighten our spirits just as bright sunshine does. If we feel inclined to complain that such paintings are crude and glaring, it would be worth while to pause and ask why we use the term 'crude and glaring' as though it were always an unanswerable reproach. Sunlight in high summer *is* crude and glaring, especially in the South.

Thousands, perhaps tens or hundreds of thousands, are grateful to Van Gogh for giving them pictures which hold so much of the sun in them, even though it proved in the end to be at an even more tragic cost to himself than the sacrifices he had made for the mining community in the Borinage.

The sun and the creative passion which would not let Van Gogh rest from painting disturbed his mental balance a few weeks after Gauguin had accepted, in October 1888, the invitation to go to live with him at Arles in a house he rented for the two of them. Gauguin was poverty-stricken. So also was Van Gogh, except for what Theo was able to send him; but what little he had was to be shared. The experiment was a failure, however. The two painters soon began to quarrel; and they also drank too much. Van Gogh threatened Gauguin with a razor in the street one night, but though he did no harm to his friend he went back home and seriously wounded himself. From that time Van Gogh became periodically insane. During the remaining two years of his life the fits of insanity recurred, until he finally shot himself, in the summer of 1890. The pictures painted in his last period – at Saint Rémy (near Arles) and at Auvers (northeast of Paris) – reflect in their style Van Gogh's mental distress. However full of gaiety and excitement the Arles paintings may appear to be, they are the work of one who had come as near to inward peace as such a man as Van Gogh ever could. It is 'rest . . . rest . . . rest' of which he makes threefold mention in the letter to Theo quoted on pp. 158–9. But after he left Arles, the earth in his landscapes seems to heave and the trees to twist as though the whole world is in unceasing convulsion: he writes in his letters of 'troubled skies . . . sadness and the extreme of loneliness'. At that time the artist's own mind must also have heaved and twisted and been convulsed. Even though they cannot here be reproduced in colour the two pictures printed on Plates 24 and 25 show the tremendous change which was brought about in Van Gogh's style as the end approached. The little flowering tree, painted two years before he died, is one of the happiest and most tenderly simple pictures any artist has made. The cypresses, painted only two months before Van Gogh's death, makes us feel as though the wrath of God is raging in the earth and the trees and the sky.

GOD – NATURE – MAN – ART

We have now reached the point in the history of art at which painters turned their backs on ways of painting that had been followed in Europe since the late fifteenth century. The Florentine painters, rebelling against the flat, stiff, formal Byzantine style, tried in every way to make their pictures as real-looking and lifelike as they could. They wanted painted people to look like real people, painted buildings to look like real buildings. To create *the illusion of reality* was one of their chief objects. Now, in the later part of the nineteenth century, the younger painters seemed to be moving around the circumference of a time-circle which led back towards the Byzantine mode. But there is this great difference: Byzantine art was governed by religious austerity, modernist art is governed by aesthetic austerity. The Byzantines served God; the sixteenth–nineteenth century artists served Nature and Man; the modernists serve Art.

A fashionable view now, among painters, is that Nature and Art are different and independent kinds of creation, and that artists are therefore under no obligation to copy Nature; that Art is best and truest to itself when it insists on independence and the right to invent its own kind of beauty in its own way. For three hundred years or so European painters had wanted to produce works of art which copied or represented Nature. We have already seen (pp. 142–3) that this is called *representational art*. Three hundred years is a very long time; long enough even for Nature to look a little stale in the works of more than a few of the later painters who continued to copy her. It was perhaps time to give Nature a rest. Representational painting had been a good thing, but once again we must remember that it is possible to have too much of anything, however good.

THE PAINTER'S AIMS

If, then, paintings are no longer to present, or represent, Nature (though the majority of them will no doubt continue to do so), what are they to do? There are two alternatives.

(1) The artist can try to *communicate* to the spectator his own private emotions and sensations – not so much what his eyes see, as the effect on his inward being when he looks at particular things. If we go out of doors on a clear starry night we may either (*a*) think that the star-scattered sky makes a beautiful picture; or (*b*) feel awestruck by the immensity of the heavens and by the thought that there are myriads of other worlds: (*a*) might lead an artist to paint a representational picture of a sky full of stars; (*b*) might make him want to paint something which would communicate to others his own sense of mystery and awe. To do the latter he would have to create from inside himself a picture inspired by the starry sky but not *like* it; not representational. It could be some awful shape of fear. In the first part of Wordsworth's great poem *The Prelude* are these two passages:

I heard among the solitary hills
Low breathings coming after me, and sounds
Of undistinguishable motion, steps
Almost as silent as the turf they trod.

. . . . . .

. . . growing still in stature, the huge Cliff
Rose up between me and the stars, and still,
With measur'd motion, like a living thing,
Strode after me.

Wordsworth was at that time living among the Cumberland lakes and high hills, and what he wrote about the effect of them upon his young imagination communicates to us vividly the half-fascinated terror he felt. It is less difficult for a poet to do this in words than it is for an artist to do it in coloured shapes. Words are a direct means of communication from the poet's mind and imagination to the reader's, but a picture gets between the painter and the spectator. If a painter produces a picture of what we have called an 'awful shape of fear' and labels it *The Starry Night*, unsympathetic and unimaginative people are likely to ask, contemptuously, 'What on earth has *that* to do with a starry night?'

In a painting such as that of the cypresses referred to on page 161 Van Gogh achieves the act of communication. He communicates to us a sensation he had himself experienced.

(2) Not all artists who forsake representational painting aim to communicate personal sensation, and we must be careful not to get into the way of supposing that these different aims are necessarily entirely separate. The greatest artists embrace them all: they are able to give us (*i*) representation, (*ii*) communication, and (*iii*) *decoration*. Many recent artists have, however, concentrated on a type of painting in which decoration is the chief factor. When paintings are no longer compelled by custom and convention to imitate natural appearances (i.e. are no longer *representa-*

tional), artists become as free to create original patterns out of shapes and colours as composers of music are to weave original patterns out of sounds and time-intervals. Though we may think it nice and friendly of Beethoven to remind us of the cuckoo in his 'Pastoral' Symphony, we do not think the less of him because such moments of naturalism (or representationalism) are rare in his music. We freely allow that a composer should make his own designs and patterns of sound. A painter is entitled to similar freedom in his own medium.

The Post-Impressionists and others who came after them wished, partly, to use painting as a means of communicating the personal sensations of the artist, but they were also very much interested in pure decoration – the making of visual patterns. If we remember that these modern French painters rediscovered the value of colour, we shall not be surprised to learn that some of them became intoxicated by it. One of the chief of these colour-intoxicated painters is Henri Matisse, who is among the most interesting and important painters belonging to the first half of the twentieth century. He has made many lovely and most careful and accurate drawings, though a number of his paintings are apparently formless. No one who loves colour should find any difficulty in enjoying his pictures, however. Although it would be absurd to suggest that his sole aim in painting is to make coloured shapes, that is how it must seem to many people. Yet even if that were all, there is much to be said for coloured shapes. If a painter makes up his mind not to copy Nature but to create from inside himself, he has nothing to create with but coloured shapes and arrangements of lines. In his employment of these he could, of course, confine himself to geometrical patterns. A contemporary English painter, Wyndham Lewis, wrote some years ago: 'There should be a Bill passed in Parliament at once, forbidding any image or recognizable shape to be stuck up in any public place.' But in practice, whether artists intend it or not, shapes have a way of taking on some resemblance to natural objects – trees or people or whatever. After all, Nature does include every shape that it is possible to create or to imagine. An artist may think that he has 'created' a shape but it is most probable that it will remind someone of a natural shape; and as soon as that happens the spectator, bothered because the resemblance is not complete, starts to fidget and complain. He does not then regard the artist as an original creator, but only as a bad imitator. He jumps to the conclusion that an ungracefully shaped woman in, for example, a painting by Matisse is simply a proof that Matisse is a bad draughtsman. Matisse is, however, a wonderfully skilled draughtsman, as we know from his beautiful drawings. Why, then, should he paint awkward-looking women?

AWAY FROM IMITATION

Most of us would no doubt agree that coloured shapes resembling a woman's figure are more interesting than purely geometrical shapes. But if an artist makes a woman's figure realistic in form, he must also make it realistic in colour; and he would then be back again at representational painting, which is just what he wants to escape from because it has become stale through too long use. So what he says is, in effect, though not in these words, 'I will take the figure of a woman [or whatever else he may choose] as raw material, but I will adapt it to my own sense of design in the way I think best. What I paint will be my own creation in form and colour: it may happen to resemble the original I borrowed from; it may, on the contrary, turn out to be quite different. I am myself the creator of this work of art, and I have a creator's right to shape the material just as I wish.'

The heart-warming and brain-stirring blaze of scarlet and yellow and blue and green and lilac and white and amber (set off by some artful use of black for contrast) in Matisse's picture called *The Amber Necklace* could be described as a deplorably crude portrait of a woman with a face that a child of five might draw. Yet how little the 'crudity' seems to matter after the first shock has worn off; and how much better it is to have this brilliantly daring and successful design in primary colours than it would be to have yet another realistic portrait of a woman added to the thousands of already existing realistic portraits of women. No one in the nineteenth century could hope, and no one in the twentieth century can hope, to make better realistic portraits than Reynolds, Gainsborough, Hogarth, Van Dyck, Holbein, Rembrandt, Rubens, Velasquez, El Greco, Titian, Bellini, and scores of others painted. To follow in their footsteps could lead to little better than imitation of what they achieved. When art follows a particular road for a long time it comes to a dead end and can get no farther that way. That is what the late-nineteenth-century French painters thought had happened, so they went back in order to find a way round. On that backward journey they met a number of forgotten or hitherto little-heeded kinds of arts. Japanese influence has had to be mentioned several times; and the younger painters (and sculptors) were much affected by African native art.

ROOM FOR ALL

Whether modernist paintings are better than, or not as good as, earlier paintings is a question that cannot be answered with a plain 'Yes' or 'No'. They are *different*, and it is helpful to know why they are different. There is no reason to claim that it is (or is not) a finer achievement to have painted *The Amber Necklace* than, say, Gainsborough's *The Honorable Mrs Graham* (National Gallery of Scotland, Edinburgh), but taste changes with changing times, and there are so many rooms in the mansion of Art that there is space for Matisse as well as for Gainsborough. We are at liberty to enjoy whatsoever appeals to our mood and our need without denying a similar right to others whose mood and need differ from ours.

About 1908, when Matisse's paintings were beginning to be better known and to seem less strange, modern painting took another new turn. It was a turn that Matisse himself disliked, and in a scolding mood he invented a word for it – 'Cubism' – which the scolded artists soon adopted as their own. As the word indicates, Cubist paintings are geometrical. Pablo Picasso passed through a Cubist phase, one of many phases in the career of an artist who has been the cause of much hot-tempered wrangling between his admirers and his opponents. Time must pass and tempers cool before his place on the ladder of fame can be decided. The Cubists became leaders in the movement towards Abstract Art, which is non-representational and almost as non-emotional as a mathematical equation. But those who find it also non-beautiful should not overlook the fact that even pure mathematics can be beautiful – to a mathematician.

BELOW THE SURFACE

The father of Cubism, though he was not himself a Cubist, was Paul Cézanne. Thirty years older than Matisse and more than forty years older than Georges Braque (the outstanding Cubist) Cézanne was the most important of the Post-Impressionists and in some respects the greatest painter during the past century; certainly the greatest since Manet, and possibly more original. After making himself well acquainted with the Impressionists' works and theories, Cézanne concluded that they were in danger of destroying something which was far more important than anything that had been gained through their study of light and colour. In his opinion they were over-stressing surface-values, and paying far too little attention to solidity and substance and structure – without which, surface is no more than a skin hiding emptiness. All Cézanne's mature paintings, whether landscapes or still-life or figure-studies or portraits, have the appearance of being solidly constructed below the surface, even though the surface is all that we are ever able to see in a picture. A Cézanne landscape makes us aware of the earth's underlying rocky structure; and behind the faces in Cézanne's portraits we feel, imaginatively, the hard bony foundation of the skull. This gives his works a three-dimensional quality obtained by a means entirely his own: he used receding planes of graduated tone (like stepped-back coloured blocks of varying size and shape) instead of conventional perspective. When looking at a landscape by Cézanne we have the sensation that we could walk into the picture and find the ground solid under our feet. Since most of the areas of colour in a Cézanne landscape are geometrical, and since the whole picture produces so emphatic a three-dimensional effect, it is not surprising that certain of his disciples should have carried the geometrical tendency a stage farther and, so, arrived at Cubism. Their journey was eased and hastened by Cézanne's statement, since repeated by others hundreds of times, that all shapes in Nature are based upon three geometrical forms – the cylinder, the sphere, and the cone. This suggests a bleak outlook on Nature, and 'bleak' is perhaps the most suitable adjective for Cubist paintings, though certainly not for Cézanne's.

THE PRIVATE VIEW

After Cubists, who adventured in the general direction of mathematics, came the Surrealists. ('Surrealism' means 'beyond realism'.) The Surrealists abandoned the field of normal vision, and concentrated upon what is revealed privately to the artist's eye peering beyond 'reality' into those dim recesses of human personality called by mental scientists 'the subconscious' – that part of us which is active in early infancy and in dreams and whenever the conscious mind (the mental and moral policeman that controls our behaviour) can be persuaded to go off duty. As Surrealism puts us in touch with a state of being which appears completely crazy to the conscious mind, though it may be perfectly normal to the subconscious, nothing much can be said about it. All of us know that dreams often appear unbelievably crazy when we are able to recollect them after we wake, yet while we were still asleep the 'craziness' was not apparent to our dream-selves. So, however fantastic a Surrealist painting may look, no one but the painter himself can judge it from any other standpoint than that of pure craftsmanship. We can say that it is well painted or that it is badly painted. That is all. The subject-matter of a Surrealist picture must always remain private to the individual artist himself. No one but Salvador Dali (a leading Surrealist painter) can possibly know anything about the peculiar nightmarish creatures (often a queer compound of human beings and chests of drawers) appearing in Salvador Dali's earlier pictures. All we can say is that he usually painted those pictures with superb craftsmanship.

So far no mention has been made here of contemporary English painters, though there have been numerous interesting ones in the past three-quarters of a century – J. S. Sargent (he was born in America but he did most of his work in England), P. Wilson Steer, W. R. Sickert, Augustus John, Stanley Spencer, Paul Nash, to name only a very few.

MODERN BRITISH PAINTERS

It is always easier to talk and write about dead artists than about living ones, because we can see their whole work and are no longer in doubt as to whether they will do better paintings than they have previously done or whether they will fail to develop, perhaps doing the same kind of picture again and again. A painter may become popular and be content to do what other people like, instead of thinking chiefly, as he may have done earlier, of painting because he had some new personal vision of nature, or could express through art something of the meaning or the mystery of life. From among the painters of our own time it will be best to choose here a few of those we can be fairly certain about, and a few others whom our descendants in future generations may add to the list of 'Old Masters' or may, on the other hand, think were overpraised by us.

An artist, even a really good artist, who has been highly esteemed in his own lifetime may be neglected for a while after his death and then came back into favour and lasting fame. For example, Wilson Steer (1860–1942) was regarded by his contemporaries as one of the great English landscape painters, worthy to be compared with Constable; but by the time he died the younger artists and art critics were more interested in other types of painting and other ways of approaching and treating their subjects. The next generation may restore Wilson Steer to his former eminence, as the present generation has restored J. M. W. Turner after a period in which he was thought of less highly.

Walter Sickert (1860–1942) seems, at least for the time being, a more important painter than Steer because he was always experimenting, and ours is an age of experimentation. He was also more interested in people. His pictures of men and women in shabby rooms, bored with one another, and the scenes in shabby yet gaudy old music halls, are intimately human but never sentimental, and they are always impressive as examples of the art of painting. Though Sickert was always interested in his subjects he was still more interested in the various ways in which paint could be put on canvas to produce different effects. In addition to pictures of interior scenes he also painted excellent landscapes and exteriors of buildings, showing in that part of his work the influence of the French Impressionists.

Like Sickert, Augustus John (*b.* 1878) is noted for drawings as well as for paintings. If there had been any scope for large wall-paintings John might have become one of the great mural painters, but he was compelled to let this side of his genius go undeveloped. He was born in Wales and became fascinated by gipsies and their ways of living, so his early work is largely dominated by that particular interest. Later he showed his excellence as a portraitist and he has painted most of the eminent persons of the period, including notable portraits of Bernard Shaw both awake and asleep. John has never been content with painting a good likeness. He tries to reveal the inner personality of the sitter and, again like Sickert, to produce a portrait which is also a good *painting*. In other respects there is no resemblance between the works of these two artists, for whereas Sickert was always reaching out towards new methods John is more traditional though never conventional and never an imitator, even when he has looked back to the style of some great earlier master. His sister Gwen John (1876–1939) painted a number of remarkable small portraits and figure-studies through which her own deep religious feeling was clearly apparent, though they were not in the usual sense 'religious' pictures.

MORE THAN THINGS-IN-THEMSELVES

With the exception of Sir William Nicholson, the remaining modern British painters whose works will be briefly referred to belong to a phase (or to phases) of art in which quite different aims prevailed. We have seen above (pp. 129–30) that 'ugly' subjects may nevertheless be transformed into great and beautiful paintings, though it is often a long while before their greatness and beauty are recognized. The ugliness, as it may seem, of certain recent British paintings comes from the artists' deliberate avoidance of the mere copying of nature. They want to paint not what *our* eyes see, nor even what *their* eyes see, but what they themselves think, feel, imagine, believe. Things then become not things-in-themselves, but symbols of other things which are too profound or too complex to be shown in plain terms of line or shape or colour. *Surrealism* is one means adopted to deal with such problems, but that is mainly concerned with dream states or with the subconscious mind. Another group of painters practises *Expressionism*, which differs from Impressionism (the representation of external things as they are seen at a particular moment) in being the representation of objects modified, arranged, or distorted in order to express or communicate some inner sensation or belief of the artist himself. Expressionist pictures are often very puzzling – as are, for example, those of Francis Bacon (*b.* 1910) and Edward Burra (*b.* 1905) – but they are probably no more puzzling to us than those of Hieronymus Bosch (*c.* 1460–1516) and William Blake (1757–1827) were to the people of their times.

Sometimes there is no difficulty at all in finding beauty in strange modern paintings. John Armstrong (*b.* 1879) can paint two leaves, one a mere skeleton of stalk and veins, against a background of what might be frozen waves, and produce a ghostlike loveliness. Or Ivon Hitchens (*b.* 1893) can brush colours across a canvas in a design that does not imitate anything at all, yet suggests deep cool forests with radiance streaming in as though through shimmering water. Or David Jones (*b.* 1895) with intertwining thin squiggly lines and patches of pale colour can suggest a remote and gentle region of myth and fairy tale.

There are, of course, subjects beyond human knowledge which a painter may treat in any one of a hundred ways without being 'wrong'. Yet Stanley Spencer (*b.* 1892) was thought by many people to be 'wrong' in painting resurrection scenes and angels in a new style and without the pious sentimental prettiness of nineteenth-century religious pictures.

MACHINES AND PEOPLE

The multiplication of machines to the present point, where they seem to be becoming more important than human beings, could not fail to affect the art of our time, so it should not be surprising, even though it may be unpleasing, to see in the works of William Roberts (*b.* 1895) men and women painted so that their bodies appear as cylindrical and rigid as great metal or concrete tubes. Industrialism of a fuller kind is taken as his chief subject by L. S. Lowry (*b.* 1887), who paints English provincial town scenes with factories and smoking chimneys, streets of small drab houses and streams of hurrying people, or loitering and lounging groups at street-corners. He is, as it were, the artist of the Industrial Revolution's after-effects, but though the scenes he depicts are dreary they are bustlingly alive.

At the opposite extreme to Lowry, John Piper (*b.* 1903) has concentrated on paintings of eighteenth-century buildings – houses, mansions, churches – either in country places or in such Georgian towns as Bath and Cheltenham. His work is rich in colour and stimulatingly imaginative, for its attraction depends largely upon skilful arrangement or rearrangement of the scenes and upon the atmosphere of a romantic past which he suggests.

The use of some particular natural or semi-natural form as a symbol to convey a spiritual or other mystical idea is fairly common among modern painters. The thorn is a significant symbol to Graham Sutherland (*b.* 1903), but many of his paintings are of a curiously-shaped object which occasionally resembles a cross between a tulip and a fly-catching orchid. He has also painted two much-discussed portraits – one of Somerset Maugham the author, the other of Lord Beaverbrook the newspaper owner – which are striking for their unusual combinations of colour, their almost rock-like solidity, and their disregard of any vanity that the men might have about their own faces. As a colourist no recent painter has been more startling than Matthew Smith (*b.* 1879), who is greatly admired by fellow-painters. He almost wallows in hot reds and other violent colours laid on with broad sweeping strokes, and is obviously one of those modern artists who love paint more than the subjects which the paint portrays. Often Matthew Smith's masses of brilliant contrasting colours seem inappropriate to the nude figures and landscapes massed on his canvases, yet even those who think them 'ugly' will hardly deny that his use of paint is tremendously exciting.

STILL-LIFE AND SHAPES

Though Sir William Nicholson (1872–1949) belongs to an older mode, comment on him has been delayed until this moment, for he excelled in still-life studies and could find beauty even in a pair of old muddy gardening boots or a pair of herrings on a plate, as well as in china jugs and porcelain bowls. His son Ben Nicholson (*b.* 1894) has carried still-life much further by confining it to geometrical patterns which appear to be no more than squares and circles of cardboard or thin wood stuck on each other and coloured. This may look a simple method – to some it looks merely lazy and silly – but its success depends upon a very exact sense of balance and proportion and upon the harmony of colour values.

DREAM-LIKE AND STILL

A few final words should be given to Paul Nash (1889–1946) who, in his last phase, practised a modified Surrealism, free from the grisly fantasies of Dali. In some of his paintings, Paul Nash's dream-world looks a cleanly-geometrical place – a sort of supernatural timber-yard which a team of hard-working and conscientious invisible charwomen might be imagined to keep constantly swept and garnished. In the same period he painted landscapes which in their simplicity of form and colour are also dream-like and still. One of his war-pictures, showing wrecked German aircraft littering the English shore during the Battle of Britain, is called *Totes*

Meer ('Dead Sea'). Perhaps it would not be unsuitable to describe these last works of Paul Nash as paintings of a dead world (another of them is called *Mansions of the Dead*), rather than of a dream world. The one selected for illustration here (Plate 27) loses a great deal of its original effect (as all paintings must) by being reproduced on a very small scale and in black and white. But at least a little of the sinister effect and deathly stillness of the original painting is preserved. It is cold and lonely and eerie, and there is something menacing about the shapes, vaguely like the bleached remains of giant shells, in the foreground. We can interpret the title, *Encounter in the Afternoon*, in any way we choose; or we may decide that it had a personal, secret meaning which died with the artist.

The Author to the Reader

As I wanted you to have your eyes and your minds entirely free for the paintings and painters I have been talking to you about, I have tried, so far, to keep myself out of sight. But now I come in front of the curtain, as it were, to say good-bye and to add that I have enjoyed writing this little book and that I hope you have enjoyed reading it.

I can't remember why I first became interested in paintings, nor why, when I was about 15, I started to go all by myself to look at the pictures in the Tate Gallery, near the bridge which crosses the Thames at Vauxhall. There I became fascinated by the allegorical pictures by G. F. Watts, a Victorian artist who painted many excellent portraits of the famous people then living, but who took himself much more seriously as a moral teacher – one of those who use paint instead of words for their sermons. When I was a boy I loved tales which had a moral at the end, and I suppose it was only natural that I should have a similar affection for Watts's pictures-with-a-moral. Not until some time later did I learn that, except as a portrait-painter, Watts was not a very good artist.

So you will see that when I began to look at paintings I did not pick the best to admire. No one had advised me what to look for in a painting; and, as I was then much too shy and timid to ask, I just followed my own inclinations. I don't think I ever heard my school teachers mention paintings; there were no good pictures in the class-rooms; and at home there were only some sentimental and soulful prints in shiny yellow maple-wood frames. (I have detested maple wood ever since!) I can never forget the picture that hung in my bedroom. It was of an insipid, tearful Roman maiden who had been offered the choice of either bowing down to a statue of the pagan goddess Diana or of being thrown to the lions. Year after year went by, and there she was, still on my bedroom wall, and still trying to make up her mind. How tired of her I became, long before I was old enough to say that I wouldn't put up with her any longer. I often wonder what became of her in the end. . . .

But that dilly-dallying Roman maiden taught me a lesson for which I have since been grateful. She taught me that if ever I earned and saved enough money to buy pictures for myself, they would have to be the kind that I could live with year in, year out, and not get tired of.

Fortunately, it was a long while before I could afford to buy pictures, and by that time I had grown out of my G. F. Watts stage. I had found in the National Gallery and elsewhere the kind of paintings which I now know one likes more and more the oftener one sees them. In this book I have tried to introduce you to a few paintings of that kind. But, while I hope that I may have been a useful guide to you, don't suppose for a moment that, while you are young, *you* ought to like what *I* like now that I am not so young. I think that my taste is now settled on a firm and reliable foundation, and it is possible that I may have saved you from floundering about for years among the second-rate, as I had to flounder for want of a guide. You must be honest with yourself, however. Don't pretend to like anything until you do genuinely like it. And remember that what you dislike this year you may come to like very much indeed later on.

It was in a roundabout way that I came at last to enjoy really good pictures. After those early visits to the Tate Gallery my interest in pictures faded. I returned to my first love – books. For several years I gave every spare moment to reading all sorts of books -- poetry, plays, novels, essays, history; for I can read, with pleasure, books on almost any subject (except money and cooking), *so long as they are well written.*

At length – after a good deal of help from a friendly and

clever little professor with enormously thick spectacles, and feet so tiny that I could never take my eyes off his polished boots – I really did know the difference between good books and bad ones. And, what was far more important, as the result of reading all manner of books I had become curious about many things outside the books. I wanted to know about all sorts of people and all sorts of things. It is hardly possible to read poetry and novels and other kinds of imaginative literature without becoming tremendously interested in life as a whole, including all imaginative art, of which painting is an important branch.

So, eventually, I found myself spending rather less time in libraries and much more time among pictures. And, to my own surprise, I became enthusiastic about a number of paintings which, previously, I hadn't liked at all. What had happened, without my knowing that it was happening, was that the reading and enjoying of good books had developed my taste in other directions also.

More than a quarter of a century has gone by, but I still enjoy those paintings. When I found that they were also the paintings that tens of thousands of other people during several centuries have enjoyed, I felt confident that I was on the right lines at last. Though I am now able to trust my own judgement most of the time, I know that any one person's opinion may go wrong. But when multitudes of people have held the same opinion for a very long time – not merely for a few months or for a year or two – you can be pretty sure that it is a sound opinion and worthy of respect. So although I have urged you not to *pretend* to like what others like, it is nevertheless good sense to compare your opinions with other people's, past as well as present.

The experience of past generations forms what is called *tradition*, and tradition has a way of being right, even though it may be healthy for us when we are young to suppose that it is wrong. The choice we have to make is often between tradition on the one hand and fashion on the other. Every

girl knows that fashions are never the same two years running. Fashion is always chopping and changing but tradition is steady; from what is new as well as from what is old
it chooses and preserves the best, and in the long run it is
from the best that our lasting enjoyment comes.

THE CHIEF EUROPEAN PAINTERS

A small *c.* (*circa*, about) before a date means that the exact date is not kno[w]

CENT.	ITALIAN	FLEMISH	DUTCH
13th *to* *14th*	Cimabue (F) *c.* 1240–1302 Duccio (S) *c.* 1260–1319 Giotto (F) *c.* 1266–1337		
14th *to* *15th*	Fra Angelico (F) 1387–1455 Uccello (F) *c.* 1397–1475	Campin 1375–1444 J. Van Eyck *c.* 1385–1441	
15th *to* *16th*	Masaccio (F) 1401–28 Bellini (V) *c.* 1428–1516 Mantegna (Pad) 1431–1506 Botticelli (F) 1444–1510 Leonardo da Vinci (F) 1452–1519 Michelangelo (F) 1475–1564 Giorgione (V) 1477–1510 Titian (V) *c.* 1480–1576 Raphael (U) 1483–1520 Correggio (Par) 1494–1534	Van der Weyden *c.* 1400–64 Memling *c.* 1430–94 Mabuse *c.* 1472–1535 Patinir 1485–1524	
16th *to* *17th*	Tintoretto (V) 1518–94 Veronese (V) 1528–88	P. Breughel 1525–69 Rubens 1577–1640 Van Dyck 1599–1641	Hals *c.* 1580–1666
17th *to* *18th*	Canaletto (V) 1697–1768		Rembrandt 1606–6[ ] Terborch 1617–81[ ] Cuyp 1620–91 Steen 1626–79 Ruisdael *c.* 1628–8[ ] De Hooch 1629–*c.* 8[ ] Metsu 1630–67 Vermeer 1632–75 Hobbema 1638–170[ ]
18th *to* *19th*			
19th *to* *20th*			Van Gogh 1853–9[ ]

e letters in brackets after the names of Italian painters show the place to
ich they belonged:
Florence; Pad, Padua; Par, Parma; S, Siena; U, Umbria; V, Venice.

GERMAN	FRENCH	SPANISH	BRITISH
ochner c. 1400–51	Fouquet c. 1420– c. 1481		
ürer 1471–1528			
ranach 1472– 1553			
olbein 1497– 1543			
	Clouet c. 1510–72	El Greco 1545– 1614	Hilliard c. 1537– 1619
	Poussin 1594–1665	Velasquez 1599– 1660	
	Claude 1600–82		
	Watteau 1684–1721		Hogarth 1697–17
	Chardin 1699–1779		Reynolds 1723–9
			Gainsborough 1727–88
		Goya 1746–1828	
	Corot 1796–1875		Blake 1757–1827
			Turner 1775–1851
			Constable 1776–1837
	Manet 1832–83		Whistler (Amer.) 1834–1903
	Degas 1834–1917		
	Cézanne 1839–1906		
	Monet 1840–1926		
	Renoir 1841–1919		
	Gauguin 1848–1903		Wilson Steer 1860– 1942
			Sickert 1860–1942
			Paul Nash 1889–1946

Index and Pronunciations

KEY TO PRONUNCIATION

| a as in bat | ā as in bate | å as in calm | ă as in ant (*pronounced very shortly*) |

e as in bet ē as in beat ė as in her
i as in bit ī as in bite
o as in cot ō as in coat oo as in soot ōō as in coo
u as in cut ū as in cute ü u with rounded
lips as in French *lune*

aw as in fawn an, en, in, on, un
(very short) (the French nasalized *n*)
oi as in boy g as in gold ḡ as ch in the Scotch *loch*

Other letters are pronounced as in English. If one syllable is to be stressed more than another, it is followed by ' (thus bak'kus). *Two syllables that are to be slurred and pronounced almost as one are not separated by a hyphen; thus* jēō *in* jēō-văn'nĕ.

NOTE. *It is not always possible to write in English the equivalent of the exact sounds of foreign words. You should regard the pronunciations given here as a guide which will enable you to get reasonably close to the versions generally considered in this country to be correct, though they might sometimes sound a little different when pronounced by foreigners to whose language the words belong. For instance, the initial sound in* Georges *is something between* j, z, *and* s, *but in a simple pronunciation scheme such as this the sound it most nearly represents is* sh *as in* shore.

A Very Famous Story

BLACK BEAUTY

Anna Sewell

ps 64

This well-loved book has now been published in Puffins. The
illustrations (one of which is seen above) are
by Charlotte M. Hough

Two shillings

A

PUFFIN BOOK OF

VERSE

Compiled by Eleanor Graham

PS 72

This anthology is intended simply to give pleasure,
and it is hoped that every boy or girl who browses
among its pages will find something to enjoy.

It ranges from nursery rhymes and nonsense poems
to verses whose meaning has to be thought about: but
whether the poems are simple or more difficult, they
have been chosen partly for that beauty of rhythm and
language which makes lines linger in the mind long
after the book that contains them has been put aside.

With decorations by Claudia Freedman

2s 6d